MY HO
OTHER HORROR
STORIES

A Mum's Funny Outlook

On Life's Ups And Downs

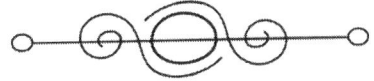

Francine G. Brazil

Copyright © Francine G. Brazil 2018
This book is sold subject to the condition that it shall not, by way of trade or otherwise, be lent, resold, hired out, or otherwise circulated without the publisher's prior consent in any form of binding or cover other than that in which it is published and without a similar condition including this condition being imposed on the subsequent publisher.
The moral right of Francine G. Brazil has been asserted.
ISBN: 9781791853945

While all the stories in this book are true, some names and identifying details have been changed to protect the privacy of the people involved.

DEDICATION

To my fabulous four.
I couldn't have done it without you... literally.
All my love unconditionally and for always.

CONTENTS

CHAPTER 1 1
CHAPTER 2 7
CHAPTER 3 9
CHAPTER 4 14
CHAPTER 5 17
CHAPTER 6 25
CHAPTER 7 31
CHAPTER 8 36
CHAPTER 9 47
CHAPTER 10 50
CHAPTER 11 56
CHAPTER 12 60
CHAPTER 13 69
CHAPTER 14 73
CHAPTER 15 77
CHAPTER 16 87
CHAPTER 17 92
CHAPTER 18 96
CHAPTER 19 99
CHAPTER 20 104
CHAPTER 21 107
CHAPTER 22 115
CHAPTER 23 117
CHAPTER 24 120
CHAPTER 25 123
CHAPTER 26 129
CHAPTER 27 132
CHAPTER 28 136
CHAPTER 29 143

CHAPTER 30	149
CHAPTER 31	153
CHAPTER 32	155
CHAPTER 33	161
CHAPTER 34	168
CHAPTER 35	174
CHAPTER 36	177
CHAPTER 37	179
CHAPTER 38	184
CHAPTER 39	190
CHAPTER 40	197
CHAPTER 41	202
CHAPTER 42	205
CHAPTER 43	208
CHAPTER 44	211
ABOUT THE AUTHOR	215

ACKNOWLEDGMENTS

To my good friend Pat Krause without whose support and technical skills I could not have completed this.

Thank you.

CHAPTER 1

I came into this world on 1st June, the same birth date incidentally as Marilyn Monroe… different year though, that's where the similarity between us ends.

She was gorgeous, I am not.

She was famous, I am not.

She is dead and I am not, although I could well be before this book ever gets finished as I've been attempting to write it for the last ten years!!

I was born the day before Queen Elizabeth's coronation (that's Queen Elizabeth the second) – my mother was asked to hold on one more day so she could get a commemorative cup, but she wouldn't and we only got a teaspoon. She was always stubborn like that, my mum. I had a four year old brother by the time I was born and my mum had already had two miscarriages by then, so I suppose I was a bit special really.

Miscarriage isn't quite right actually as mum's first pregnancy went full term but unfortunately resulted in a stillborn baby girl. That probably wouldn't have happened these days but I'm talking seventy years ago. The second miscarriage was at six months, between my brother and me, and that too could possibly have been saved these days. The wonders of modern science, eh? Well I might have not been here if those pregnancies had resulted in living babies. My mum only ever planned on having two children so there we are… and here I am.

We had a happy childhood, me and my brother. Looking back it wasn't exceptional in any way but I always have fond memories of my childhood regardless. I remember playing out in the street a lot with my brother – no amend that. He didn't ever want me hanging around and wouldn't let me join in anything but I watched him and his friends a lot from the side-lines and his friends were always really nice to me. I don't think they dared not be, he was a toughy, my brother, even back then. But undeterred by his total indifference and irritation with me I followed him around relentlessly.

We did interact occasionally, me and my brother, like when I'd go into his bedroom long before he was ready to wake up and lift his eyelids up to see if he was awake. I suppose that could have been a tad irritating for him, especially as I did it most mornings. I've always been an early riser! He used to then get me to count his marbles which were kept in an old school PE bag. At the last count there were 3,763 as I recall. I wonder whatever happened to them. Sometimes he agreed to play with me when it was too wet to be outside with his buddies. Kids didn't have friends in the house to play much back in the day, not in our house anyway. He said he'd only play if we went into the 'best' room. Now this was a room that rarely saw any activity, for some reason it just didn't get used much. In fact I only remember it getting used when my dad bought a snooker table to go in there. My dad and brother were both avid snooker players and watchers. My dad passed away over ten years ago but snooker was his passion to the very end of his days. Even on our little black and white television set my dad could differentiate the colours which in itself is miraculous as he was colour blind with red, brown and green, something that has in fact been passed on to one of my boys, but surprisingly, he never got it wrong.

Anyway, on this rainy day my brother agreed to play with me in that 'special' room. Now I hated that room, partly because it always smelt musty probably due to the lack of use, but the main reason I hated it was because I couldn't reach the door handle and was always afraid of being locked inside. Ludicrous really as my mother was always around and I had a good pair of lungs when it came to shouting out loud and it wasn't a mansion by any means. Anyway… my brother knew I didn't like this room but that was the only condition he would play.

Now I bet you're thinking that you know exactly where this is going, but no, you'd be wrong, he didn't leave me in that room by myself and run off having slammed the door firmly shut, leaving me screaming, as had happened on many previous occasions, and yes I did still trust his assurances that he wouldn't do that again. Naive or optimistic or just desperate for him to play with me? I don't know. But no, on this occasion the plan was to ride around on each other's backs and race around the room. It was great, he ran around on all fours trying to get me to fall off and I was hanging on for dear life. Loved it. Then it was time to change around and he would go on my back. I was a bit reluctant to change over, as I said he's four years older than me and was a lot heavier even though I was always a stocky child!! So we agreed he wouldn't put his full weight on me, but of course he did, making my hands bend back completely and I totally passed out.

There was another time we happened to be in this dreaded room, looking out for my mum who'd just popped to the local shop, which was all of about three minutes away. But while she was gone and I was pressed up to the window waiting her return (she never left us so this was unusual and scary) my brother kept repeating over and over that she'd never be coming back and that he'd seen her packing a suitcase. By the time Mum got back I was a gibbering wreck and I think he got a clip round the ear for that one.

Then there was the time I happened to be sitting on top of a very shiny round topped brick wall. How I ever got on there is a mystery looking back, but once on, I didn't know how or dare to get off. In steps my trusty brother, arms outstretched telling me to just fall forward and he would catch me. After a few failed attempts to 'just fall forward', I finally plucked up the courage and 'fell forward' by which time my brother must have got fed up or something and he stepped back, leaving me to fall flat on my face and break my nose. To be fair he did have the good grace to take me back to our house, saying repeatedly that I should never trust anyone.

Oh, happy childhood days…

CHAPTER 2

We lived in a small, back to back house in a street opposite my paternal grandparents for the first eighteen months or so of my life. Of course I have no recollection of that time. My only memory of that little street is when visiting my grandparents one time when we'd moved away from there and being given a key for the communal toilet three doors down and I swear that key was a foot long! I also had a couple of aunts and uncles on that street too, that's how it was back then. Although I can't remember any of that time they were happy times for my mum and dad with family around them, and looking at old photos of street parties and communal get togethers it did look idyllic.

My grandma died when I was three years old and visiting ended. I think my grandad was a gambler and a bit of a womaniser and my dad had very little to do with him once his mother passed away. My mum was the youngest of seven children and her oldest sibling was more than twenty years older than her. Her mum and dad came to Britain from Russia at the turn of the 20th century. My grandad came over first to find work and lodgings and his wife and two-year-old son followed. It must have been heart wrenching for my grandmother to travel to England knowing she would never see her mother and sisters ever again… she was nineteen years old.

My maternal grandmother died when my mum was only sixteen so of course I never knew her, but I wish I had. I think she had quite a sad life really. My mum said she often heard her crying at night missing her mother, sisters and homeland. My grandad worked at night as a baker and was a lovely kind gentle man. He passed away when I was eleven and I remember him quite clearly. He lived in England for more than sixty years but never lost his strong Russian accent and always drank his tea black through a sugar cube held between his teeth. Funny what you remember.

CHAPTER 3

My parents owned, well, not owned, but were buying their own home and when I was about ten they decided to move house into a better area with more space and a bit bigger garden. I had a little sister by then so we needed to 'upsize'. My mum had never intended having any more children but when I was eight and my brother was twelve she became pregnant with my sister. She was beside herself, actually, as she was thirty-eight by then and felt too old to become a mum again. People generally had their kids much younger back then and I think she was acutely embarrassed. The doctor at the time had told her she was in the early stages of the menopause and not to worry. So, my sister was born in 1961, my brother was mortified and could only cope with the idea of a baby in the house if it was going to be a boy. Looking back I think both my mum and dad were through with that stage of their lives and maybe didn't have the same energy they'd had for me and my brother.

So there we were, excited and ready to move house. Three bedrooms, bigger garden, nicer area... then the bombshell dropped, and my dad was made redundant.

In a way it's strange that I ended up living most of my life in England, I suppose. My dad was a tailor by trade and in the early sixties there was a slump in the tailoring trade. He found it difficult to find work. The planned house move had to be abandoned of course but as our own house was virtually sold my parents decided to continue with the sale and took up the government's offer of £10 passage to Australia. Of course I was totally unaware of all the implications of this major upheaval. I was just really excited about it. We had been to Australia House in London and all the necessary i's and been dotted and t's crossed. All we had to do now was to wait to be given a date to sail to our new life in the sun. My parents had been advised that we would be setting sail in about six weeks' time. In preparation my parents sold all our worldy goods and possessions and we all – my parents, me, my brother and sister, moved in to my aunt's house to wait it out.

Unfortunately things don't always go to plan and because of the bad state of the country at that time, many families had decided to take up this £10 offer of a new life and we were informed that our wait of 6 weeks would more realistically be in the region of 18 months. This news came as a shock and caused a bit of a problem actually as my aunt, who only had a two-bedroomed house, was about to be re-housed herself and her house was due to be demolished within six months.

Oh, dear!

My God, living in that house must have been a nightmare actually. There was all my family, me, my mum and dad, my brother and sister, and my aunt, uncle, my two cousins and my grandad. How did that all work? I remember two boys sleeping in the bathroom, there was only one toilet and that was outside in the yard and I think my uncle moved out! No-one liked him much anyway. Bloody hell, I'm going to stop talking about this – it sounds like I lived in the dark ages and it's depressing me. So, we had to be re-housed so that my aunt could move out and her house knocked down. Mustn't stand in the way of progress.

Unfortunately, as we'd made ourselves homeless, we didn't qualify for one of the newly built redevelopment properties further out of the city where there was grass and trees and space that my aunt was going to. No. We were firstly offered a subterranean basement flat, which my mother refused to accept, saying my dad had been a prisoner of war for two years (which was quite true, he had) and that they were not going to live in a basement. We ended up in a house in the red light area of the city.

We never did make the move to Australia and I've never visited there. Maybe one day…

My poor parents, what a hard time it must have been for them. Instead of 'going up' in the world or starting a new life at the other side of the world, they were having to start again with no money. Any savings had been used in the months my dad was out of work, no belongings of their own and three growing kids to support. Awful really, and it makes me sad to look back on that time as an adult, and to realise to some extent how terrible and stressful it must have been for them. For me, it was fine. In fact it was more than fine, I didn't have as far to walk to school and my best friend lived three doors up. We would phone each other constantly when we weren't together. My dad used to tell me to stand on the doorstep and shout instead. Of course I never did.

My dad had found employment by this time but it was out of the city and he had to be up at the crack of dawn to get two buses in order to arrive at work by 7.30am. He didn't own a car, my dad, which was just as well really as he'd never actually taken a driving test. He apparently had just been issued with a driving license while in the army. We did get a car eventually when I was about seventeen, perfect timing I'd say, and my dad sort of taught himself at the wheel.

CHAPTER 4

I didn't enjoy my early school years, I didn't enjoy school much at all really, but my very early years set the tone, so to speak, for the rest of my school life. I always felt anxious and nervous to varying degrees throughout my school days.

My days at infant school were particularly dreadful. My strongest memory is of one teacher who really seemed to dislike me. I was quite a bright child and could tell the time and write before I started school. But this particular teacher never let me answer a question when I put my hand up, in fact, she totally ignored me unless it was to tell me off. I was never a naughty kid – I was just too scared to be but she always seemed to find a reason to be angry with me. I think it was just because I was there!

There was none of this softly approach back then and kids were sat at tables according to their ability. This teacher put me on the bottom table with the real numpties and the kids with candle snot permanently hanging from their top lip. I knew, even at that young age, that this was an injustice and I hate injustice.

You were never allowed to go to the toilet unless it was break time, and because I was so scared I always needed to go. There was this one time I just couldn't hang on 'til break but being so scared of the teacher and knowing I'd never be allowed to go to the toilet even if I'd asked, I just wet my pants. I did think I'd get away with it as we were standing at easels painting at the time and there was lots of water about, but no, she knew what had happened but just didn't know which vile creature had done it. She said in her stern croaky voice that if no-one owned up she would come round and feel all our pants. Petrified and hardly able to speak I stammered that it was me. She was disgusted and made me sit on my own in my very wet navy knickers for the rest of the day. By the time school finished those now dry navy knickers were like cardboard. I remember my mum going in to school about that episode and the bitch of a teacher just chose to mainly ignore me totally for the rest of my time in her class. I was five.

I soon learned to keep a low profile, something I've practiced for a large part of my life.

There was another incident involving a toilet while I was at infant school. The toilets were outside in the yard where we played at break times. You had to be pretty quick to get back to your class on time, particularly if you decided to go nearing the end of break time, or if there was a queue, which there always was. So there I was running up the stone steps to get back to my class before break time ended, trying to place only one foot at a time on these just too big stone steps. I fell, cracked my head open and had to go to hospital and have stitches. But my overwhelming memory of that is not the hospital trip, not the injections or the four stitches I needed, but is that of the headmistress coming out of her office, which was situated halfway up on these stairs, and asking me repeatedly if I was running, which was against the school rules. She went on to be head of a girls' correction centre.

CHAPTER 5

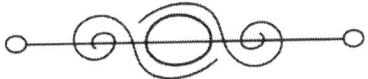

The years went by and me and my friend started going to the Youth Club, a bus ride away, we would have been about fourteen then. We went two or three times a week and would have gone every night if we'd been allowed, we loved it.

Our dads would take it in turns to meet us off the bus at 10pm because of the kerb crawlers that were out and about in our area. We regularly missed the bus we were supposed to get which left either her dad or mine waiting anxiously a further half hour. We just found it hard to drag ourselves away from the place. Of course our parents had no means of contacting us, or us them. We were just thoughtless, weren't we, and we didn't even feel that bad about it. Everything just seems funny when you're fourteen.

Me and my friend spent most of our time in her bedroom in those days messing about, or should I say experimenting, with make-up, talking about boys and laughing uncontrollably. All the while eating ham and piccalilli sandwiches with plain crisps and listening to The Kinks – 'Lazing on a Sunny Afternoon'.

My friend's older sister's boyfriend worked as a rep for a make-up company and we had lots of free samples to experiment with. It was great. I remember one time we really got adventurous (or carried away in the moment) and in addition to the usual foundation, eyeshadow, blusher, mascara and lippy we decided to draw eyelashes on our faces. Feeling very artistic we went down to my house to show my mum our handiwork. My dad, normally a quietly spoken, extremely tolerant man, uncharacteristically for him, was really angry and told us to take it off and that we looked grotesque. He possibly thought we looked like the ladies of the night that frequented our area. We used the word 'grotesque' a lot that summer, me and my friend, and fell about laughing each and every time.

We would go out feeling like we looked so good and individual in our matching green leather three-quarter-length coats and our matching black patent vanity cases with our matching pink chiffon scarves tied on to them. We didn't restrict our experimenting to make-up only. Oh no. We coloured our hair on a regular basis, we went from Rimmel red to blue black and every shade in between. There was this one time we had a go at perming my friend's hair. She fancied a few soft curls. I don't remember quite what went wrong but suffice to say she wasn't happy with the outcome. The curls were so tight and springy and it looked absolutely shocking. We were going to the cinema that evening, they were showing a different scary horror movie every night for a week and we wanted to see them all. She had to cover her head with a scarf so we could go out, hoping the curls would soon drop, before anyone we knew saw it. Unfortunately as the curls were so tight and springy the scarf was no match for them and as she stood in the queue for ice-cream from the usherette in the interval under the glaring spotlight, her silhouette was priceless and well suited to the horror film we'd just gone to watch.

Back then we still sat the eleven-plus exam and my friend passed and went on to grammar school, while I apparently was borderline. The headmistress called my mother in to school to discuss what to do with me. It was agreed that I should not go to the grammar school where I might be challenged and struggle but be sent instead to a newly opening secondary school where I would sail through easily. Big mistake in my opinion.

Apart from me not knowing a single soul and having a fifteen minute walk to get a bus on an unfamiliar route to this place… 'secondary' was true in every sense of the word. A lot of the teachers were, in my opinion, second rate and not very interested in their chosen profession, and the kids were drafted in from all the roughest areas of the city. Not their fault and everyone needed to be placed somewhere but I didn't feel I belonged there and found it difficult. Luckily for me, I had perfected the art of keeping a low profile, I'd had a lot of experience at it. I did, however, sail through easily. I never had to put any effort into my work, I always stayed in the top sets and don't recall struggling academically at all. What a waste…

I didn't stay on to do my GCSE exams as I couldn't get away from that place quick enough.

So what to do next? According to the careers advisor who spoke to me for a full four minutes, my choices were limited.

Choice number one: get a job in a department store

– they were always looking for staff.

Choice two: have a baby and get married – or the other way round – this was implied rather than suggested.

Or

Choice three: (if you had any illusions of grandeur) go to college and train to do secretarial work.

I chose the latter.

I enjoyed my time at college, even though taking the shortcut home through the park on a dark winter's night could be a bit scary and on one occasion a man in a long coat exposed himself. Astonishingly, and although I wasn't particularly good at PE, I managed to run like the wind on that occasion. Shame there was no-one around to see it.

I liked the step up from being at school and the way the teachers spoke to you. It felt much more adult being there and I loved the work too. I even managed to enlighten one or two of my new friends that Jews were quite ordinary, like them, and didn't have horns coming out of their heads. They found it a revelation. Hopefully it had some impact in their later life – who knows?

Of course, like many university students now I

expect, the fact that you've got a certificate and a qualification you might imagine the world is waiting for you and you breeze into a top job. I naively assumed I'd be using my newly acquired skills and be some important person's private secretary! What a disappointment. At sixteen the only job available to me was that of office junior. Only right and proper, of course, but back then it was a bitter blow.

It was very easy getting a job in the late sixties/early seventies. You could walk out of one on the Friday and have another to start on the following Monday – something I did quite regularly. I found office life generally very tedious. The usual tasks of making tea, filing, running errands and generally being everybody's dogsbody didn't suit me at all and I hated it. I loved the typing side of the job when I got the chance to do that but didn't like being the 'gofer'.

To be fair though, I have always had a strong work ethic and at thirteen my first Saturday job was at Leeds market on a fish stall. I don't think you could really work at thirteen but market life was quite relaxed and if you said you were older nobody checked, nobody cared. It was great. Me and my friend both got a job on this fish stall and we had a ball. It always surprised me though how many women would ask us if something was fresh or ready to eat –

like we knew!! We were thirteen for goodness sake – what did we know about fish? Nobody particularly wanted to sit next to you on the bus journey home, can't think why. But that only added to our enjoyment.

I graduated from fish to fruit and veg, and I loved that too. I've always like the free and easy style of market life and the camaraderie that goes along with it. My mum, a big market shopper all her adult life, would come along once a week for all her weekly fruit and veg requirements. She'd give me a pound note and I would give her nineteen shillings and sixpence change.

I must have had more than two dozen office jobs in total trying to find one that suited me. I stayed at some for a few months and one or two I only managed a morning. I did have one office job, though, that I loved. Mainly I think because it was a new business just starting out and two very gorgeous guys from Liverpool owned it. The atmosphere in the early days wasn't formal at all and we laughed and joked a lot. That suited me really well and we got on great. I stayed there quite a while, over two years I think, but it grew in size and became very successful, luckily for them, and that meant it had to become more structured and as that didn't suit me quite so much, I became restless and decided to leave.

All through my office years I was paid weekly in cash, which I think many people were at that time. Me and a few other office worker friends would usually meet up on a Friday lunch time and treat ourselves to a Chinese meal from the 'set menu', which was very popular at the time. The menu changed weekly but the food always tasted reliably the same.

I eventually came to the conclusion that perhaps office work wasn't for me. I always felt a bit like a square peg in a round hole so to speak. Not wanting to be out of work I took a job clearing tables at a coffee shop. I rather enjoyed it actually, having banter with customers and being much more relaxed than office work, but I knew it wasn't for me and was just a time filler 'til I decided what to do next. My mother was a tad disappointed her daughter had a job clearing tables and was pleased when I decided it wasn't a career I wanted to pursue.

CHAPTER 6

I passed my driving test at eighteen years old and my dad by this time had a car. My driving instructor was a kindly middle-aged man who thought I might be better in the back seat - with him – rather than behind the wheel. You'd be arrested for saying something like that these days, but having worked in offices for a couple of years, you got used to hearing lots of these kinds of comments, and worse, on a regular basis, so I just ignored it, and I passed my test first time.

I used my dad's car A LOT back then and as long as he was left with enough petrol to get to work the following morning, he was pretty relaxed about it. Because I often used to get home in the early hours and because there weren't too many cars on the road back then, I used to be constantly stopped by the police and asked to show my documents at the local police station. In fact it happened so often that they only had to see me at the police station door and told me to go without checking my documents. I remember driving to London one Sunday and for the entire journey hardly seeing another vehicle on the recently opened M1 motorway.

I suppose I was a bit of what you'd call promiscuous back then. It was the sixties after all, and of course the inevitable happened. At seventeen I became pregnant. I knew absolutely that I wasn't going to have a baby, quite honestly the thought of it was ludicrous to me, so I went to see our local doctor about having a termination.

Abortion had only been legalised a few years earlier, thankfully for me, but at that time I hadn't as yet told anyone about my situation – and I was scared – sick to my stomach scared. I'd decided to sort things out on my own as far as I could so that when the news broke I would be well on the way to having resolved the situation. I didn't have to tell my mum in the end, she guessed I might be pregnant by my whole demeanour.

I needed two doctors' signatures to enable me to have the procedure and as my GP who'd known my whole family for years was ill, and as I was in a hurry to get my situation sorted as quickly as possible, I decided to call at his home. After all, I only needed his signature. His wife answered the door and I nervously, but resolutely, told her why I was there. She was furious but I was determined to get his signature and she reluctantly managed to get it for me. It was arranged for me to attend a private clinic out of my home city. My dad gave me the money I would need to have the procedure. The only comment my dad made was to say, that one mistake was an accident, but two mistakes of the same kind made you a fool. So I set off alone to get the train to my destination, I was full of trepidation. I had to get a taxi at the other end as I didn't have any idea of where I was going and I was taken to a private clinic where they were expecting me. I had the procedure and stayed overnight there then made my return journey home, and nothing was ever mentioned again. I never regretted my decision and went on to have four wonderful children, when the time was right.

At about nineteen years old I was once again very restless, I didn't know which direction my life was going and was depressed. I decided to go to the

Middle East. I'd found a scheme where you could go to Israel and live on a kibbutz for a year, the plan was to work in the morning and then in the afternoon, you'd have lessons to learn the language. There had been an assurance back in England that any young adults going on this scheme would be kept away from the more potentially dangerous areas. If and when you completed your year out there you would be given a return ticket back home. I was really looking forward to going although I was very nervous as I was doing this on my own but it was through a legitimate organisation and everything was arranged; travel, accommodation, and even being met at the airport at both ends. My dad drove me down to Heathrow airport where there were another four people from different parts of the country that had also signed up to this scheme. Happy days.

On arrival in Israel we were met by a pleasant enough chap who took us to his open backed vehicle which was to take us to our new destination. Now I knew quite a few people who had done a similar thing to me over the years and their description of the places they were 'billeted' to had sounded great. There had been tennis courts, a cinema and even swimming pools - a regular holiday camp, or so I thought.

The place that was to be my home for the next

year was bleak. It was situated on the border with Jordan and armed guards patrolled at night. No tennis court, no cinema and no swimming pool. In fact we discovered milk and eggs were only available on Tuesdays! As each kibbutz is self-sufficient and as there were only a hundred or so permanent residents there, it was quite poor. But no matter, I was in a beautiful country with lots of sunshine, so let the adventure begin.

I was given a variety of jobs to do whilst I was there. One time I'd be in the vineyards pruning grapes, or picking grapefruit, which incidentally are lovely and sweet when first picked, and we'd often eat one on our morning break. Another time I'd be cleaning the doctor's surgery or sitting on a tiny stool with a bucket of water and a scraper, cleaning newly laid eggs in the hen house. I didn't mind any of the jobs I'd been allocated.

What I did mind, however, was having to attend weekly meetings that were spoken only firstly in Hebrew and then translated into Spanish. There were many Argentinians and Brazilians on this scheme that had travelled from their home countries – but only five of us from Britain so it wasn't considered necessary to translate or cater for so few. The problem was that as we were on the scheme, we had to attend these weekly meetings even though we couldn't understand a word. Not attending was not an option as that was the rule. If you were on the scheme, you went to the meeting. In addition to hating injustice, I equally hate rules just for rules' sake, especially when they are plainly ridiculous and make no sense whatsoever. In fact it really infuriated and frustrated me.

I did really enjoy most of my time there but got fed up with the hierarchy and silly rules so left after only four months and returned back to England just after my twentieth birthday.

So back home and job hunting once again.

CHAPTER 7

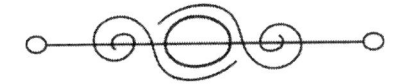

I checked out the job section of the evening paper every night to find something I wanted to do. Clearly office jobs were a non-starter, been there, done that. Then I spotted a vacancy for a 'relief' collector, clean driving license required. Yes I thought, that could be for me – I loved driving. The company who had advertised the position was out of town and I arranged to go for an interview. The job was to empty fruit machines that were situated in pubs. My job - if I got it - was to cover rounds throughout the North of England and North Wales when the regular collectors were on holiday or off sick. I really wanted that job and I'd get a company car! The interview seemed to go well I thought until we got to the part of having a clean driving license. When I had said my license was clean it wasn't exactly true, I had a few points on for speeding offences. I was gutted because I really wanted that job and I knew I'd blown it. I came away from the interview feeling downhearted, it had sounded perfect for me. I went back to looking in the paper for a job but my heart wasn't in it as I'd so wanted that job. Then a few days after my interview I got a phone call saying I'd been successful. Unbelievable. I was over the moon.

I loved that job, there was a fair bit of training involved, as each pub landlord received a percentage of the machine's takings. This varied from brewery to brewery and also depended on whether the landlord was a manager or a tenant, all of which had to be worked out by the collector on site. Obviously it wasn't possible to get around all the calls for the day outside of pub opening hours, so I'd often be sat at a table for all to see, surrounded by heaps of coins to count in full view of customers. Mostly customers were pleasant enough but on occasions there were some that weren't happy that you were taking all their cash.

As I was a relief collector I had to first travel to the area I would be covering, then find all the pubs on my round for that day. In the days of no satnav, each girl whose round I was covering wrote out all the directions for me to follow that I would need to get me from pub to pub, in what were always unfamiliar areas. Back in the day, I was just grateful for a magnetic clip that I could stick on my dash board to attach their handwritten directions to.

Trying to read handwritten directions in an unfamiliar city whilst driving wasn't an easy task. To add to this sometimes the directions were inaccurate. It might say, turn right at traffic lights, for example when they had meant left, an easy mistake to make I dare say but it might take me a mile or two to realise things weren't tying up, but at which point had they gone wrong? A bit stressful at times, I can tell you, especially as I also had to complete my round, cash up all the money I'd collected that day from the machines (in my car with the doors locked - and most of it was in coins) and get it to the bank before they closed around 3 o'clock!! In spite of the trials and tribulations I still loved that job, and sometimes it even meant staying away overnight in a nice hotel when I was say, in Wales, lovely.

As I said navigating my way through a busy unfamiliar city centre whilst following written directions wasn't always easy and I had a fair number of little knocks and bumps in that company car but the firm had its own garage to maintain and repair their fleet of cars, and I was a regular visitor. On day one of my new job and training completed, my first calls were to be in Sheffield. I found the first pub on my round quite easily. I parked outside, gathered the things I'd need, took a few deep breaths and braced myself to enter the premises. I opened my car door… and bang, a passing bus took it clean off, I do wish drivers would take more care!

Generally I managed pretty well and once I'd got more familiar with the rounds I covered it obviously got easier, although covering a seaside resort in the height of summer was always going to be a challenge. There was only one place where it got a bit more nerve-wracking and it was at a pub in Liverpool. This particular pub was well known in the area and any decent person would have to be pretty desperate for a drink to have ventured in there. My instructions were to radio into the local office when I arrived and a member of staff would come and sit in their car opposite the pub, probably to see if I got out alive. I had to park my car on the pavement right outside the window while I was inside. The machine in there was the only one I ever came across that had a steel bar and padlock on the outside – and it would still often be empty more often than not when I opened it. I loved that job. I only gave it up when I became pregnant with my daughter and lifting all that heavy cash was going to be a bit too much.

CHAPTER 8

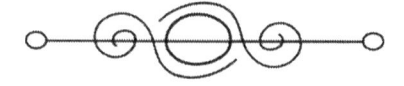

My daughter was due in the June of 1979 and my husband and I married in the January of that year. We had been living together for a couple of years and were buying our own house together so it was a natural step with the baby coming.

I realised sometime after our wedding, though, that I'd married an alien, like most women do, I suppose. Obviously we spoke the same language but somehow by the time my words reached my husband's ears the meaning had been lost somewhere in the ether. I think it works like some sort of code that was used in wartime, where the message gets scrambled en-route but unfortunately he was never able to de-code it. Things might have worked out better had we just stayed as we were and not felt the need to get married, who knows? It was probably me that didn't fit well into the box of married lady, I put certain expectations upon myself that I couldn't easily adapt to.

However...

Looking back, the die was cast, I guess, on our wedding day. I had decided to wear a black flowing affair with large orange flowers printed on. I know. But let me say in my own defence at this point, I was three months pregnant and I reckon that could have seriously affected my judgement in the clothing department. Anyway, it was a very cold January day the day we married and it had snowed the previous night. Now our driveway was steep. Very steep actually and also very uneven. So negotiating said driveway on a lovely sunny summer day, in perfect daylight and wearing flat shoes was tricky. So trying to negotiate that driveway on the morning of our wedding, in January, covered in snow, wearing strappy heels and clutching a bunch of flowers was never going to be easy. Funny that we both left from our own house, it hadn't occurred to either of us that I should have perhaps stayed at my parent's house the previous night as was the custom. No matter. So that hurdle overcome, we gathered at the register office and duly got the deed done. I was very nervous actually when it came to the repeating of the vows part of the ceremony. Although it wasn't funny in any way at all, for some reason I could hardly say my piece for this awful laughing fit that had taken hold of me. I think it was to do with the solemnity of the occasion, I've always been a bit like that. You know, everyone is sitting po-faced and serious at some really solemn event and then this bubble starts to rise within me and my shoulders start to shake and I daren't catch anyone's eye or I'd lose control completely. The thing is, it makes you come across as quite an uncaring person and I'm not. I just find it difficult to take serious things very seriously.

So there we are, wedding ceremony over, my cousin had taken all the snaps we needed and off we went to the restaurant for our 'wedding lunch'. We had decided to have a simple affair and get a new kitchen instead of a bigger do and no kitchen. It sounds rather grand doesn't it, to say 'new kitchen', well it did to me back in 1979. These days it would be some super-duper jobby from Möben kitchens or similar. Ours was going to be flatpack job from MFI that my new husband was going to have a go at putting in himself.

So... I'm in the car with my husband and my now

in-laws when my lovely mother-in-law asks her son where we are staying on our wedding night. My husband says mysteriously that it's all been sorted. He wouldn't be drawn on any further details but I was nevertheless quite excited, and impressed, as I hadn't realised he'd organised anything. Well, meal over – I'd ordered T-bone steak, which was odd really as I'd completely gone off meat at that stage of my pregnancy - so, meal over and we are on our own in our hired car. We only had a mini-van and it wouldn't have been appropriate. We set off towards York, me badgering all the way and wanting to know where we were going. He was still being very elusive. We stopped at a lovely hotel and I started to get out of the car. My husband got out and said for me to stay in the car for now. No vacancies!! Nothing had been booked as he just hadn't thought about it, and only said it had been organised to placate his mother. I have to say I was a tad disappointed at this point. So we trudged from hotel to hotel in York, in January, in the cold and couldn't get in anywhere. York was full!! I was beginning to feel a little like Mary in days of old. No room at the inn.

We travelled on to Harrogate, surely we would find somewhere there. We did eventually find a place that took pity on us and squeezed us in a little attic room but by this time I had started with awful toothache so none of it really mattered. The moment had been lost. The next morning we decided to set off back home to Leeds. It had been drizzling constantly, that fine drizzle that can really make you feel depressed unless you are on something to blot it out. We put our meagre overnight bags in the boot of the hire car but couldn't figure out how to close the hatchback and spent a good ten minutes in the rain trying to figure it out. Still, onward and upward.

I decided to revert back to using my own name after about ten years of marriage. I hate the phrase 'maiden name', it conjures up an image I just don't feel comfortable with. I had never felt like myself using someone else's name. Maybe it's just me but I felt like I'd lost myself and felt like me again when I went back to using my own name. I suppose it's a good thing that most women don't feel the way I do or there might be complete chaos and government might have to legislate, like they do for most things, to enforce women to take their husband's name when they marry. It was funny actually because when I started using my own name the kids also started to use my surname. So school had to be informed and forms filled out etc. As the news that our name had changed began to filter through, I would get strange and quizzical looks from women who I'd seen at the school gates for years but had never spoken to. You know the situation where you see someone regularly but you never actually acknowledge each other the first time or two of meeting, so you then have to avoid eye contact thereafter, and there is a kind of wary uneasiness whenever you pass each other. Well, one or two of these woman actually approached me and asked if I'd re-married as my name had changed. They were nice women in actual fact. Nosey but quite nice. But all those years of jostling and evading each other's eye were over so that was a good thing. Incidentally everyone started to call my husband by my name, having assumed that it was his name that I had taken. Funny that. He didn't mind.

We are not together now, me and my husband… two reasons really. Firstly, he passed away in August 2014 but prior to that, in 2007 and after almost 30 years of marriage I decided we should alter our living arrangements and see how things went.

I decided to move out of our marital home for a while and I had the opportunity of moving into a small terraced house for a few months. It had been something I'd thought about for a number years on and off and when the opportunity came along I took it. I hoped this might make me realise how much I really wanted to be back home and that my husband might wake up to how great I was. Alas that wasn't to be and in fact we both realised we were perfectly fine on our own. Well I'm not being fair here actually. I realised I was perfectly fine on my own and that truth be told I preferred living alone and felt quite liberated. I don't know how my husband really felt about it as communication wasn't ever our strong point, but hey ho! I moved out of our marital home temporarily in September 07 and rented a house from a client of mine. Let me just explain the term 'client' before anyone flatters me by jumping to the wrong conclusions. I owned a small nail and beauty salon in the suburbs of Sheffield and this lady had been coming to me for a number of years. We'd become quite good friends, so when she decided to go on her world travels with her partner for a few months, she was more than happy for someone to be in the house until she returned rather than it stand empty, and it was the perfect way for me to test the water so to speak. I moved in on 1st September 2007 and absolutely loved it from day one. My sister came to stay for a week the day I moved in and although her leg was in pot from toe to knee and she had some very tricky manoeuvring to perform to negotiate the very twisty stairs to get to her bed in the attic bedroom, we had a great time. Truth be told, I think she was rather reluctant to leave. In fact most of my married women friends who visited me there loved it and wanted to stay indefinitely! For me it was a brief taste of a life I had missed out on. I had gone straight from home with a shared bedroom with my sister to being married and sharing a bedroom with my husband. Funny thing is, having shared a bedroom with my sister for all my life until I married, I have absolutely no childhood memories of her in my life until we became adults. I wonder if that means something.

Anyway, I went to work as usual and went back to my lovely little house. I didn't do anything spectacular. I didn't do the things young people might do when they first have a taste of freedom. Just being there and just being on my own in my own space was wonderful. Me and my husband still went out for tea as usual on Friday evenings (we still split the bill) and I usually went back to our home on Sundays for lunch and the kids would all usually come round with their families as they'd always done and it wasn't a big deal for anyone. The kids had known I'd been unsettled for a number of years and as they were all grow up, this was just about me and their dad, and we were all still together, it was just that the living arrangements had altered temporarily.

I'd spent a lot of my married life feeling suppressed and to be fair this wasn't entirely my husband's fault (a lot of it was, ha) but it clearly wasn't all him. It never is all one person. But it's often difficult for a person to feel equal and strong in a relationship when you have young children dependent on you and you have no income of your own. No money equals no power, and that's not a good place to be. Some women are much better at adjusting to that situation but for me I felt totally disempowered, insignificant and demotivated. Moving into that little house started to take me back to the person I knew I was.

Actually the change back to myself started when I went to college at the age of forty to do my very first ever GCSE, but more of that later.

So after seven months of living on my own, and after a lot of soul searching and a bit of counselling I made the decision to make the arrangement more permanent and I moved back home and we put our house on the market for sale. Living back at home was difficult in the wake of what was about to happen. My husband had truly thought my moving out was just some 'woman thing' and that normal service would be resumed. He was truly devastated about his house having to be sold. That was part of the problem I guess... his house. Thankfully, the house sold quite quickly and on 10th October 2008 both me and my husband moved into our respective new houses. We stayed married and lived only a few roads away from each other. It worked well for us. We chatted, we saw each other, we'd do favours for each other and we'd spend family time together with our children and grandchildren. We'd both then go to our own home where we could both indulge in our own little ways. I moved into my new home on a Friday and on the Sunday my very pregnant daughter, her husband, their three-and-a-half year old daughter and their dog moved in with me. It worked really well. I had a house and no furniture and they had all the furniture etc and no house. A match made in heaven.

Funnily enough our moving day was probably one of the most enjoyable days me and my husband had spent together in years. We laughed a lot and hugged and decided who got what. I wanted very little as I wanted to get all new eventually and my daughter and family were initially moving in with me with all their belongings. Temporarily. I clearly remember our removal guys commenting on the fact that we seemed unusually friendly to say we were splitting up and that they had never witnessed anything quite like it in all their removal years. I preferred to think of our separation more like an altering of our living arrangements rather than splitting up. After all we had been involved in each other's lives for all of our adult lives and we had a lot of shared history, we were always going to remain a big part of each other's lives, just in a different way. So there we were, all his things in the van first, my bits and pieces at the end so we could unpack me first then go on to his, all most enjoyable really, a good day, and then we went out for tea together (it was Friday). We split the bill which seemed only proper now – funny though, we'd always done that

So that was it. We lived apart but shared lots of things together, like travelling to Cardiff to visit our son and his family and three little boys. He fixed things for me and had my door key when necessary to let people in to do jobs when I couldn't be around due to work. He usually ate at mine on a Sunday when the family came round and it all worked well. In fact we probably enjoyed each other's company more than we had done in the last thirty years.

CHAPTER 9

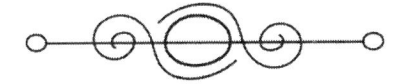

At the age of forty I decided to get an education. Let's not get carried away here, I just decided I'd have a go at getting a GCSE certificate. I'd left school at fifteen without taking any qualifications and went on to college to do a secretarial course. As I previously mentioned at my school there were limited options, work at Woolies, get married and have kids or get on a secretarial course. I chose the secretarial option. But by the time I'd reached forty I felt I was getting left behind.

My kids were all doing, or about to do, their GCSE and 'A' level exams. My husband had a degree from Leeds University and I felt I needed to prove something to myself. I enrolled at college and did a

GCSE in English language and literature. I passed it easily enough with a high grade and went on to do my 'A' level in the subject. I could have continued on from there and gone on to do an access course to get into university but I felt that I'd done what I'd set out to do… and yes, I could have done uni if I'd had the opportunity and the right advice at the time, but that ship had sailed and with four kids it was now more important for me to earn money and give us a bit better standard of living and help my husband provide for us all.

For a number of years I had done childminding, not because this was a career choice, but needs must and with four kids of my own I needed (and wanted) to earn money and that seemed to fit the bill. At home for my own kids and earning some cash at the same time. Perfect. But as my kids were getting older and as they were becoming more independent I had to plan for my future and decide what to do with the next, probably last third phase of my life. I knew that because my kids had been my whole life for years that if I didn't find something to do I would have this great void in my life and I wasn't going to be one of those mums who just lived through their kids and sat around waiting for grandchildren, so I had to decide what to do next. It was at this point in my life I was slowly starting emerge from some kind of tunnel and become myself again. It was as if I had been living an alien life sometimes and I did occasionally wonder how I'd got the life I had. But after going to college and with my kids becoming more independent I felt I was becoming liberated and it felt great. I've loved having my kids and obviously still do and would never have ever chosen another way but like everything in life it come at a price and for me that price was that I had to lose myself for a few years and devote myself to them and their wellbeing. But now, here I was becoming me again because I was able to take some control back of my life and make decisions about which way it would go forward. When you have kids their needs have to take priority over your own, I believe, and somehow life just evolves, but now I could make choices again and it felt good.

So what next... what did I want to do… what could I do?

CHAPTER 10

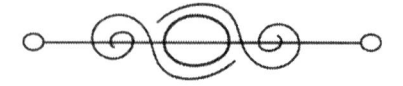

I started my own nail business in 2000. I had never in my wildest dreams thought about owning a business. I had just decided when my kids reached a certain level of independence and maturity that I needed to plan for my future, so I chose to do what interested me and what I loved - doing nails.

Firstly I had to learn how. My plan of action was to firstly go to a salon and get my own nails done. I asked lots of questions whilst I was there but only got guarded responses. I guess the staff had been instructed not to give away any trade secrets! Undeterred, I then sat in my car and made notes on what had been the procedure as far as I could remember. I booked in to the salon a number of times until I felt I had enough information to give it a try myself. I had some business cards made and opened an account at a local trade warehouse and bought what I thought I had seen being used in the salon. I then spent many an evening practicing my new-found skill on any friends that would let me – often with painful and disastrous results. My poor daughter would eventually only let me use one or two of her fingers to practice on as she could no longer bear the pain!

Eventually I felt I was competent enough to be let loose on the paying public, so I placed ads in the local shop windows and waited for my phone to ring. It was scary going to do those first ladies' nails, I can tell you. I had my newly bought kit plus quite a heavy lamp to take along in case the lighting where I was going wasn't adequate. Looking back it's a good job I didn't realise how much I still had to learn. Thankfully ignorance is bliss. Those poor ladies sometimes had to be at my mercy for up to four-plus hours and by the end I think we'd both lost the will to live. Suffice to say I never got any repeat bookings from those early clients.

Undeterred, I answered an advertisement placed in a window on a newly opening nail salon that was looking for nail technicians. The owner of the business was male who actually knew very little about doing nails, I think he wanted it as a 'babe magnet'. But fortunately for me my knowledge was slightly more than his and I seemed to satisfy the criteria so I got the job as a part-time nail technician. Luckily for me the other newly appointed full-time staff member was very experienced and she was incredibly helpful in honing my skills into something much more polished, pardon the pun, and professional. And there I stayed for eighteen months. Between us we were running the whole salon as the owner only rarely put in an appearance so it was a natural next step to go into business for ourselves and open our own place.

Our salon opened on 3rd January 2000. All went well for the first year or so. We were building up a good client base and were getting busier by the day. We soon realised that we would need to take on extra staff as we were both working flat out most days. We started having problems when it came to staff as they found it difficult working with my business partner, who could be very abrupt and unpredictable at times. Needless to say, apart from one or two loyal wonderful girls, staff came and went at an alarming rate, culminating in only being left with one girl, who stayed and was wonderful. But clearly something had to be done, as apart from losing good staff, our client base was also starting to diminish. Unfortunately, again I discovered this was due to my partner's manner. They say a partnership is the hardest ship to sail I'm told and so it proved to be. So after four years together in our salon we had to have a parting of ways. I took over the business and my partner moved on to open her own salon in another part of the city, closer to her own home. I have never seen or heard from her from that day to this, which is a shame, but I will always be eternally grateful to her for the help she gave me in the early years.

I always thought that owning a business, like so many things in life, was for 'other' people. But you know it really feels so ordinary and natural. Don't get me wrong, I love it, having the salon, but it does feel normal, if you know what I mean. Funny though how people always assume that when you have a business, no matter what it is, that you are in the money. Actually the girls that work with me often earn more than I do! But I love the work I do. All the girls enjoy it. It's not really like work, it's more like a glorified coffee and therapy session. You would not believe some of the stories we hear in the salon. Sometimes a new client comes in and as soon as they sit down with you it's like a tap has been turned on and you get an hour of the most intimate details of their lives. I'd almost work for nothing, it's so fascinating.

In fact it's having the salon that made me think of writing in the first place. Every time you get another funny/interesting/sexy story from a client I'd think 'you could write a book' or 'you couldn't make this up'. Actually the nail salon would make the most perfect sit-com, I don't know why it hasn't been done. And if the clients didn't provide enough material to keep it going for at least a decade, then the girls that work there certainly could. Some of the things they came out with are priceless. I remember this one time I was preparing silk to be used in the salon and this involved tearing it into strips initially. I happened to say that I felt a bit like Florence Nightingale preparing bandages. Two of my girls looked at me with a bit of a vacant look on their faces and asked what I meant, and who was she? Did they know her... was she a client?! I gave them a very brief resume on her and they looked at each other and decided that they must have been off school the day they did her.

There was this other time when we were chatting about various things and I happened to say how awesome and fantastic I had found Stonehenge when I visited there some years before. Now there is a huge outdoor market not too far away from Sheffield that opens from about March to December and is a very popular place to visit. It takes approximately thirty minutes or so to drive there. Well on this day, one of my girls said, 'yes I've been to Stonehenge but it didn't find it that special'. I was a bit surprised that she wasn't awestruck by the whole atmosphere and magnitude of the place as I had been and asked her when she'd been. She said it had been a couple of years ago, on the way to Thoresby Market. I insisted that whatever she had seen I could promise her it hadn't been Stonehenge. She was quite positive that it had been and rang her husband for confirmation. She wasn't on the phone very long and she never did tell us his response. She did say that what she had seen was most likely Cresswell Crags. An easy mistake to make and very interesting in their own right I'm sure, but they ain't no Stonehenge.

CHAPTER 11

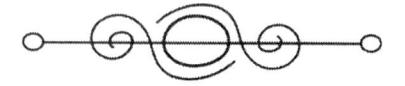

Did I ever tell you about the time my friend, the one who worked for the airlines at the time, wanted to take me to Paris for the day for my 40th birthday? She used to get a number of free family and friends passes so thought it would make a really nice treat to give me a bit of a special day out. I've known this friend for almost all of my life and she is great to be with and quite a powerful lady. She has had a very successful career and I always thought that if she'd gone into politics she could have been Prime Minister. She decided many moons ago not to have children and as such our lives travelled on very different paths for a number of years. However, we always kept in touch and our friendship has always remained strong. Now that we are both middle-aged we have once again got much more in common and still enjoy each other's company immensely. I remember when my kids were all very young she would sometimes breeze into my house in one of her many fox furs (it was ok then) and stilettos and we would chat just as we had always done. Me in my grow-bag leggings, no make-up and unkempt hair and up to my knees in kids and nappies, you couldn't have found a more seemingly incompatible twosome. But it never made any difference to us. I do recall, though, when she'd gone on her way I would be a bit down and ever so slightly envious of her lifestyle. My husband, who wasn't particularly sensitive as a rule, would notice a difference in me and asked if my friend had stopped by. I told her about that once and the funny thing is that when she arrived home to her husband, he used to ask her the same question… funny that.

Well back to my 40th birthday treat. Back in the day I didn't have a passport of my own but was on my husband's passport as his spouse, but it meant that as he was the main passport holder I couldn't travel without him. That's how it was then, and he certainly wasn't included in this trip. Luckily I had heard about a travel document you could buy from a main Post

Office for only a few pounds that enabled you to travel for up to twenty-eight days but you had to state your country of destination. No problem... *France, please.*

So there we were at Leeds Bradford Airport, only it was called Yeadon Airport back then, early in the morning so we could get as much packed into the day as possible. She, of course, was very cool, while I on the other hand felt really excited as this was a big deal for me, going on a day trip by plane! But I tried to also appear cool as if this was routine for me too. Then there was an announcement that there was fog in Paris and that flights had been delayed until at least midday. My friend suggested that we might go to Amsterdam instead if it didn't matter to me, no fog there and we could set off almost immediately. It didn't matter to me.

We boarded the flight and drank Bucks Fizz and sat right at the front of the aircraft. Not right at the front as in the cockpit with the pilot, although I would have loved that but felt it too childish and uncool to ask. But on the front two seats. You know, the ones you always wished you had been allocated on a package flight but never are. About fifty minutes later we landed at Schiphol Airport. We had just passed through passport control, really looking forward to the day and I was promptly arrested. A stern-looking woman, I think it was a woman, in military style uniform and with all kinds of metal-wear hanging from her belt appeared from out of nowhere and took me accompanied by my loyal friend to a back office. Her English was not all that good and my… whatever it is they speak in Amsterdam, well whatever it was I wasn't fluent in it, but no matter I was bullet-proof, I had my travel document. I rummaged about in my bag and produced this piece of paper which enabled me to go to… France!! Bloody hell. There was a lot of noise and a lot of gesticulating and my buddy made a couple of phone calls and we were allowed on our way. A bit of a hairy moment though, I can tell you. I have my own passport now and travel wherever I want, whenever I want, but it was an experience neither of us will forget and we still laugh about it to this day.

CHAPTER 12

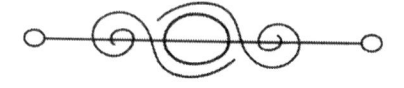

Then there was the August Bank Holiday of 2004. I took my daughter, who was then twenty-one, to Paris for the weekend. I booked us on a coach trip as I figured it would be a more relaxing and stress-free way for us to travel and see the sights Paris had to offer. *Mistake!!*

We boarded the coach at our local pickup point after me checking with anyone and everyone in the near vicinity that it was in fact the right coach for us. There were so many coaches about all waiting for their human cargo and I didn't want to get off to a bad start. It's so easy to end up on the wrong one!! We settled down in our allocated seats, that was all ok, then a very large woman waddled down the centre aisle with a very skinny man bringing up the rear, struggling, being loud, dropping things and generally making a huge fuss as they headed towards their seats. I just knew exactly where they'd be heading, very near us. They had lots of carrier bags with them, which looked suspiciously like my usual weekly supermarket shop and as soon as they had boarded the coach I just knew they'd be sitting somewhere very close to me and my daughter. They were directly behind us. Firstly they seemed to take a full inventory of all the edibles they had brought with them – I think they were planning for the journey ahead. Then they proceeded to chat, chew and rattle their way down the motorway. By the time we had reached Leicester Forest I felt like putting my foot in her mouth. My God it was irritating, but as ridiculous as it sounds we found that we were actually concentrating on everything that was going on behind us. So as well as being extremely irritating it also became very, very funny and every time there was another rattle of a sweetie paper or when she was mad at him for not passing her something that she wanted quickly enough and accused him of trying to starve her, me and my daughter almost fell about laughing. It got to the point where me and my daughter couldn't even look at each other or we would have just lost all control of ourselves. It's not easy travelling all the way to Paris in such a state, I can tell you. We were exhausted by the time we arrived. But arrive we did.

We eventually arrived at a very mediocre hotel – well not an hotel exactly – more of a travel lodge type place. So we all get off the coach, stretching and thankful to have arrived whatever the accommodation. We are all congregated in the lobby having been shepherded in by our travel guide (I had forgotten how much I hated this aspect of coach travel), and we are all waiting to be given our room keys. Keys are being handed out and people are wearily filtering out of the lobby, when it becomes clear that there is a problem. There is only me and my daughter left remaining in the lobby and it's not looking good. The receptionist is doing a lot of shrugging and head shaking and our rep guy is looking and sounding a bit vexed. The upshot of all this is that we don't appear to have been allocated a room. After much discussion and looking at lists and finger pointing it becomes clear what the problem is. Our names, it would appear, had been right on the crease of the fax sent to the hotel/lodge when our travel company made the booking and we had therefore been overlooked. At that precise moment a middle-aged woman from our group (who had been given a room incidentally), walked determinedly back to the reception desk to demand a better room. She was angry and said it wasn't right that her aged mother had to sleep in a pull down cot-type bed as there was only one 'proper' bed and that it just wasn't good enough. You bloody well sleep in the pull-down, I thought, you mean bitch. Apparently this was the style of twin room in this place. I very kindly offered her to swap with us. She looked interested until I informed her we didn't have a room at all!! That was us out of favour with her for the duration of the trip.

Now it seems that the 'allocated' seats on the coach were only necessary for the outward and homeward journeys, so that's UK to France and France back to the UK, so me and my daughter chose other seats whenever the coach took us to the centre of Paris or indeed on any other excursions we went on with the group. Let me tell you this went down like a lead balloon with the other passengers. You should try it sometime. We humans are creatures of habit, aren't we? If you have ever been to, say, an evening class you must have noticed that whichever seat you first choose remains your seat for the duration of the course. Upset that at your peril. By the time me and my daughter were on our return to the UK I think we'd managed to alienate ourselves from just about everyone else on the coach – and all because we had sat in different seats. For some reason this also seemed to complicate the obligatory head count we had to undergo each time we boarded the coach!

My daughter had decided we could do our own sight-seeing independently of the tour wherever possible. I must say I was a little less keen – but hey, two independent women, we'd do 'our own thing'. I was a little apprehensive when we first ventured out alone. We arrived at the metro to get a train to take us to the centre of Paris. Now, we were staying on the outskirts of the city in a less than salubrious part of the city. The metro station we were at was patrolled by an armed guard and the whole area looked decidedly run down and seedy. But undeterred, we managed to buy a travel ticket that enabled us to jump on and off the metro about a dozen times throughout the day.

I was absolutely hopeless, I must say, and relied solely on my daughter's ability to figure out where we were, when we got on and off and where we were going. We did extremely well actually – up and down – on and off - lattes here, cappuccinos there, felt quite confident by mid-afternoon when we decided to visit the Sacré-Coeur and Moulin Rouge. Once again back on the metro, we got off at the correct stop and emerged in to a place where to say we stood out like sore thumbs was an understatement. We decided to act cool and nonchalant and not draw attention to ourselves, this was not as easy as it might sound as we were clad head to toe in touristy type trappings, camera, designer bags, sunglasses etc... but I think we carried it off!! The Moulin Rouge was a bit of an anti-climax for me actually. I expected more, or different, anyway.

Well, all sightseeing done for the day we boarded the metro once more to get back to our original starting point and back to our accommodation. At this point we were both a little weary and slightly confused as to where we were supposed to get off and indeed in which direction we should be travelling. After a few minutes working it out and feeling reasonably confident that we'd managed to sort it (neither of us speaks or reads French apart from the usual *s'il vous plaîts* and *mercis* – so not an easy task), we suddenly saw what we thought was the station where we had first boarded the metro earlier that day. We jumped up and got off.

Now all day we had been putting our travel tickets into the machine, gates released and we were able to get in and out of the subterranean metro system. So there we were back at our station, or so we thought, at the end of our journey, almost back. Great! My daughter put her ticket into the machine. Big solid eight foot high steel doors released and she escaped. I put my ticket into the machine... nothing. I tried again, and again... nothing. So what to do now. It's late, it's quiet and it's getting dark. My daughter is on one side of these steel doors and I am on the other and the place is deserted. There are no staff to be seen and no other passengers appear to be around. Bloody hell. I am looking at these steel doors and I can't get out and she can't get back in. There is a gap of about eight inches at the bottom of the door and I am seriously wondering if I could squeeze through. My daughter on the other side was starting to feel a little unnerved. She told me there was a fire burning in the middle of the street and what she described sounded rather tribal and not like Paris at all. Acknowledging the fact that there was no way I could get through an eight inch gap (even if I held my breath and sucked everything in) and brute force on the steel gates having had no effect whatsoever I decided that the only way was to try and climb over the top. My daughter is sounding increasingly nervous as a group of youths are looking her way and one or two are starting to saunter in her direction. Right, I have to do this, I thought. I have to get out of here and get to my daughter. At that point a foreign gentleman emerged seemingly from out of nowhere, muttered something about Egypt, and tried my ticket for me in the machine – several times. Clearly to no avail, I'm not a complete loon, I'd tried that, and he sauntered off. Alone again. By now I'm feeling quite desperate and am psyching myself up to do a superhuman leap over the steel gates, when like a miracle a spotty youth, deciding obviously not to pay for his journey, forced the steel gates from my daughter's side and we were reunited.

Relieved to be together again once more we soon realised, however, that we were not where we ought to be. To be fair, we had done quite well and seemed to be in the general vicinity but as our day metro pass seemed exhausted we started the long trek on foot back to our hotel. A couple of hours later we were back at our hotel. We were absolutely exhausted, starving hungry and generally bedraggled, but we put on a brave face and told our fellow 'coachees' we'd had a great day and that we preferred exploring on our own. We reached our room and collapsed on to the beds. I didn't think my legs would ever move again as they'd turned to jelly and we were too late to eat! Incidentally, one trip we did go on with the group took us to a sort of hospital rehab place and the tour guide told us that if we were lucky we'd see an invalid in the grounds. We were not lucky on that particular day – but we managed to get over the disappointment!!

My daughter had met a new boyfriend (now husband) a few weeks before our Paris trip and spent a lot of time on my mobile talking and texting him. I think my mobile phone bill turned out to be more expensive than our weekend away. Mind you, that phone bill didn't compare to the one I had after the two week holiday me and my husband took to Skiathos – the one where I had diarrohea, sausage legs and fell through the canvas chair and gauged my back, yes, that one… oh, haven't I mentioned that one yet? Later…

CHAPTER 13

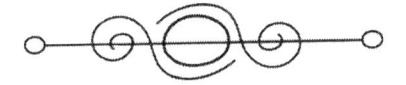

There was this one time we went on a day trip to St Annes, near Blackpool. We had actually gone to lay the ghost of a previous holiday there which hadn't been too successful or enjoyable. We'd gone for a week in the September and I don't think me and my husband spoke until the Christmas after that one, but I'm getting ahead of myself. The day trip.

Everything had gone quite smoothly really. The kids ranged from two to seven at that time, so even the car journey there was going to be a bit fraught potentially. You know the usual plans for a day trip with kids. Firstly I was up at about 5am to make the picnic, it's expensive eating out for six, and there are no fish and chip shops in St Annes, well there wasn't back when we went. So, sandwiches were to be made, drinks needed to be sorted, and the usual treats had to be packed. One bag for the car to keep the kids quiet (come on you all do it), crisps, bananas, juice, the sort of things that can be easily accessed and hopefully keep things calm for the duration of the trip without making them feel too nauseous. It's a fine balance. Then there's wipes for sticky fingers and faces, sing-along tapes (no CDs then). The boot is crammed with the picnic proper along with buggies, changes of clothes, nappies, towels, swimwear, buckets and spades etc.. all the usual stuff for a day trip. It's now 7am, I feel like I've done a day's work just preparing for the day and then the kids start drifting downstairs. Breakfast before we go, nothing too heavy. Everyone washed, dressed and ready for the off. We all pile into the car. This pre-dates the compulsory wearing of seat belts. Just as well really. We had our four wedged in like sardines in the back seat, no-one was moving anywhere. The usual jostling for position, apart from the youngest as I'm sure she was in a child seat if my memory serves me correctly, until Dad intervened and told everyone exactly where they were sitting. So off we go. The kids are excited, hubby is in control of the situation and I just want to go back to bed quite honestly. So we survived the journey and the morning on the beach without too much trouble. My usual permanent holiday migraine hadn't kicked in yet so it was a good day. As we strolled around the town area my husband decides he needs to get a newspaper. Why would you need a newspaper and when are you going to read it with four young children on a day trip? I stayed with the kids while he shot across the busy road to a newsagents. By sheer good luck we were opposite a NatWest Bank.

My youngest wanted a wee. So making sure the three older kids held on to my skirt and not taking my eyes off them for a second, I pulled down my daughter's tights (it can get really chilly at the seaside) and swept her legs from under her and squatted down over a drain for her to have a wee. Unfortunately, what she had meant was that she had actually already done a poo. As I'd been keeping my eyes and attention on the other three, I'd not been looking at what I was doing with my youngest. Shock horror. My daughter now had poo, which looked suspiciously like the egg mayonnaise sandwich she'd partially eaten at lunch, all down her legs and down the left sleeve of my rather nice cerise pink sweater, one I'd thought quite flattering, actually.

I couldn't stand up as we were both in such a mess. I looked around in panic, desperately needing my husband to make an appearance pretty pronto, but he had evidently gone to Blackpool for the newspaper and was probably sitting somewhere bloody well reading it!! He seemed to have been gone ages. Then like a miracle someone came over from the NatWest Bank which was actually closed to customers as it was after 3.30 and banks had normal closing times back then, and asked if we'd care to use their toilets as they'd been watching from a window and saw what a state I was in. Talk about a caring bank. Unfortunately the pink sweater never recovered and I've never been back to St Annes. Actually I kept up a brief correspondence with someone from the bank for a time, me thanking them, them responding and me replying back, but it had to end, I felt it was going nowhere.

CHAPTER 14

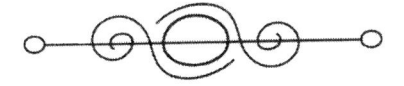

My sister came to stay one time for the weekend. She had left Yorkshire and gone to live in Norfolk... I know... she ended up living there as she had met the right man who happened to live in the wrong place!! At least as far as I was concerned. I use the term 'right man' loosely as I'm not convinced there is such a thing, but maybe I'm just a bit cynical. Well it was not actually a weekend. She arrived late Saturday night and left Monday morning. It was one of her flying visits so to speak. We only seemed to manage flying visits which was a shame really. I love her lots, which in itself is odd as she is very gorgeous and really slim. She is eight years younger than me and has always been a head-turner. Actually there have been at least three separate occasions during our adult life when I have mistakenly been taken for her mother! Something she has found hysterically funny, I never found it quite so humorous. In fact I'd go as far as to say it's deeply wounding actually. People can be so cruel can't they? Anyway I love her nevertheless and in my own defence when these absurdly ridiculous comments were made I was considerably heavier than I am now and I suppose I could have looked quite matronly, and on one occasion I was heavily pregnant and so not looking at my best.

I did manage to shift a couple of stone at one time way back, with the help of Weight Watchers. Around that time I had a birthday looming and was kind of hoping not to get any chocolates, but thank goodness my then two year old granddaughter had the wonderful idea to buy me some. Thornton's… yes!! I'd just have one or two perhaps, I thought, and stay in control. I knew how to do that now. After having eaten almost all the top layer and with a mixture of both relief and disappointment in equal measure I realised there was only one layer…

We went on holiday together once, a week in Majorca, me and my sister. My youngest daughter had her fourteenth birthday while we were there. My sister took her two girls and I just had my youngest girl with us; 'a girlie one'. Of course my sister looked fabulous – all the time – while I tried to keep up and failed miserably.

On the day of my daughter's birthday we'd discreetly organised a cake to be brought out after we'd had dinner at our hotel that evening. As we filled our plates from the buffet with the usual mix of meat, fish, meatballs etc as holidaymakers do, a complete mish-mash as you can never decide what to have and it all ends up looking like a dog's dinner, and then tastes the same every evening (not my sister, I hasten to add), we kept nervously glancing about us to see if this cake would make an appearance. Food eaten and trying to kill time until said cake showed itself, no mean feat in itself with three girls eager to be off to the mini disco I can tell you. Salvation. At last a person who looked like a member of the kitchen staff emerged struggling with a cake that looked like it could have kept a small village in the Sudan going for months. Unfortunately, she passed our table and wandered around the dining room looking somewhat bewildered. I don't know if this was from the weight of the cake or she just didn't know where she was supposed to deposit it. We tried to distract my daughter from this floor show which had started to catch the interest of the other diners. As she came our way I felt relief that she'd found us and not spoilt the 'surprise'. Unfortunately, she passed us by and went back to the safety of the kitchen. A minute or so later she re-emerged. By now it was clear my daughter had sussed what was happening so as the woman looked like she was going to pass us by one more time I called, 'here, love, I think that's for us', in my best broken English so she'd understand. By this time any attempt at subtlety and discretion had long gone. But the cake was lovely and we all managed a small piece and left the remainder for the other three hundred or so diners.

Things always seemed eventful in one way or another when we went on family holidays. I say holidays but prefer to think of them more like a test of endurance and if we passed we could stay at home for the next fifty weeks. Going on holiday in the early days with four children aged five and under was never going to be easy. The one year me and my husband went on holiday just the two of us was no less eventful than the years of going with the kids.

CHAPTER 15

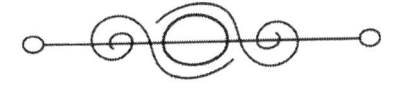

As it had worked out, all of our four kids would be away whilst we were on holiday, so it had been a simple matter of running down the food stock in the fridge and generally leaving everything neat and tidy for our return. All nice and orderly, that would make a change!

Our eldest daughter was on a six-month trip around Europe. She had taken her younger sister with her. My youngest daughter was seventeen then and had her eighteenth birthday in Rome – how wonderful! I felt quite confident about them travelling together as my eldest girl had been travelling round the world for about two-and-a-half years prior to this European jaunt so she knew what she was doing.

Their plan was to travel through Germany to Poland, visit Prague, then Italy and eventually get to Greece where they had lined up bar work for the summer. On route to Greece however they had contacted their brother who had a good job working as a duty manager in a very trendy sports bar in Sheffield and persuaded him to join them for the summer. That took all of two minutes!!

The day my son was due to fly out to join his sisters he was totally comatose from saying his goodbyes the previous night to friends and work colleagues. He must have had a good night as he had 'GOODBYE' written across the width of his back in red felt tip pen which he had no knowledge of. He just kept giggling and seemed quite bemused to be told that he had a flight to catch that day. But rouse him we did, eventually. He must have still been hungover as he made his way to board the flight as he had apparently left his passport and boarding card on the table where they'd sat to have a coffee while waiting for the flight to be called. His dad had to make a mad dash back to where they'd been sitting to retrieve the documents and just managed to intercept a cleaner who was just about to pocket them. The last piece of the jigsaw was that my youngest son who was at university would meet up with all three of them in

Greece during his lengthy summer vacation. So they were all sorted and we would be back well before any of them returned to the UK.

We had gone to the Greek Island of Skiathos. We had decided to go self-catering so we could 'please ourselves'. The accommodation was simple but it was adequate for our needs. Two weeks of absolute nothingness. How wonderful. We did decide to go on a couple of trips as we couldn't 'do nothing' every day. On about day two of the holiday however I got the most dreadful diarrohea, something I don't normally suffer from. Well I don't suffer with much really. I am lucky in that I rarely get ill but on the seldom occasions when I do, I am really ill. Anyway I've got this problem and my husband insists that I get something from the local apothecary to help. Well I'm not good in foreign countries, I feel totally out of my comfort zone and having to ask for something for diarrohea, how embarrassing is that? I thought I'd just choose something from off the shelf to save any embarrassment in having to try to explain my problem. Unfortunately nothing was familiar to me so I just bought a disposable camera. Realising this wouldn't be of any help with my condition, unless I intended to take pictures for any future claim, once again I had to go back into the chemist shop. This time my husband came in with me and did all the gesticulating necessary to get the appropriate medication. That wasn't the end of it. No. On about day eight of our hols my legs started to swell. They got so bad that they looked like huge sausages and I thought my skin might burst. I had to spend the whole day lying on my bed with my legs raised. All I could do was lie there and read a book. Thinking about it, it was a very pleasant day actually. When does a mum of four get to lie down all day reading and being undisturbed, and feel absolutely fine? I sometimes used to daydream when the kids were a lot younger that I might get just a mild bout of something that might put me in hospital for a few days. Nothing serious of course and certainly not life threatening, but just a few days away from it all, meals served up and no one to bother you. Please tell me I'm not alone in this! So on to the day trip.

It was going to be a long day. We had to start at 6am as we needed to first get a boat to the mainland. This might be a good time to point out that my husband isn't good on boats. Anyway, we then had to board a coach to take us some six hours' drive away to our destination. I wanted to sit near the front of the coach so I could look straight ahead, it's awful isn't it if you can only see the surrounding countryside with your head at a ninety-degree angle to the right or left? So let's say I set quite a good pace from getting off the boat and getting to the coach. I didn't set any marathon record for this of course and my life didn't depend on where we sat but I was just a bit single-minded in getting from boat to coach. You know how most holidaymakers are, sauntering about looking around trying to catch some likeminded soul to make a friend of for the duration of the trip. Not me, I do all the socialising I need in my work life and with my ever expanding family. I don't go on holiday to make friends.

So there we are, first seats behind the driver. Perfect. Then along comes this bull of a man, who I had spotted earlier as I'd made my way to the coach. Huffing and puffing, he plonks himself down with all his video equipment on the adjacent seat. Well at last all the stragglers arrive, having aimlessly sauntered along, and all took their seats. The guide and driver then arrive. The guide firstly tells the 'bull' that he and his timid looking wife have to sit elsewhere as the seats they are in are reserved for her - something I'd been aware of from the outset hence my choice of seat. Well he starts billowing and blowing and saying that he and his wife can't change seat because his wife gets travel sick. Why go on a six hour coach trip for goodness sake?!

"Tell them to move," he says looking at me and my hubby. Not on your life mate, I'm thinking. "I get sick too," says I, "that's why I chose these seats at the front." He had to move but he wasn't happy. He had wanted to video the whole of the six-hour travelling along boring roads. That would have made interesting viewing for the folks back home, wouldn't it? He looks at me with complete rage and moves to a place further back on the coach. A couple of hours into the journey I heard him sounding off as his video camera had run out of juice. Moron!!

I did have another minor incident during this trip. About halfway into the journey we broke for a comfort break - toilets and refreshments in layman terms. I sat on a chair in the sun while my husband went to get us some drinks. It was a director style chair. You know the type. Metal frame with canvas back and seat. Well I'm sitting there in the sun when the canvas totally split and the rusty frame gauged my back. Now as I've previously mentioned, I've always had a bit of a weight problem, but honestly it wasn't down to me. I think that chair had been there since the first Olympics judging by the state of it. Anyway, I got up quicker than I went down I can tell you, and thank goodness the bull's video camera had given out, he would have loved that one!!

There was just one other minor incident during that holiday, but it was back at the apartment (ha – apartment). When I say apartment, it was just a basic room really with everything just about squeezed in. I'd just come out of the shower. You know how the floors are all tiled, and you know how slippy they can be? Well I went full length. It was miraculous actually. How I only sustained a badly bruised elbow and an egg on my head I'll never know. Just lucky, I guess.

Now I don't know how or why me and my mobile phone became the conduit from which all the communications between my globetrotting kids seemed to have to go through that summer. Maybe it's that old habits die hard and I have always and still do have a large involvement in my kids' lives. So, we had been on our hols for a few days, all good so far. I perfected the way of greeting fellow Brits and then turning away so they would realise I didn't want to meet them on the beach or go back to sit on their balcony and have a drink with them and hear all their very boring stories about bathrooms/wall ties/family etc. I'd fallen victim to that before. Then the first call came through on my mobile.

Firstly my girls needed to contact their brother to alter the meeting place they'd organised. The bar job they thought they'd organised hadn't materialised and they'd found work elsewhere, as in a different location geographically! Not being able to contact their brother my youngest daughter had gone to meet him at the airport to intercept him. They unfortunately managed to miss each other as he hadn't been expecting a welcoming committee of one and as such just left the airport. Meanwhile my eldest girl had finally made contact with him when he landed but then couldn't get hold of her sister, who in turn didn't know whether to hang around the airport or return to base. I'm getting all this whilst relaxing on a beach in the sun supposedly. No wonder I had the runs!!

By the time my youngest son flew out to meet them, which he thought had been arranged, but they thought was only a maybe, they'd decided to move on as they'd had enough of being cheap labour and wanted to go to Amsterdam. Because of return flights and seemingly intricate travel plans best known only to them, the girls flew to Amsterdam but their brother had to fly back to Heathrow, get a coach to Stanstead airport then fly out to Amsterdam to meet up with them again there. Just about this time, their brother had arrived in Greece.

He was really disappointed as he really wanted to go to Amsterdam but stayed in Greece for a few weeks and did a bit of work to keep himself going.

When he got fed up with that he decided to join his siblings in Amsterdam. Unfortunately the other three had run out of cash, hadn't been able to find any work and decided to return back home - one problem - no one had a door key, and me and their dad are still away on our hols. In amongst all this chaos and globetrotting, money had to be transferred between bank accounts etc, and all done on my mobile phone! The three travellers eventually arrived back home to a house with very little food and no money between them. Their brother, meanwhile in Greece, disappointed to have missed out on Amsterdam boarded a flight back to the UK. Unfortunately he had flown into Newcastle airport and with no means (money) of getting back to Sheffield his brother had to drive up to get him.

A few days later me and my husband arrived back home. Remember I said the house had been left neat and tidy? Well the girls had been away for six months, the boys had also been away for weeks and there had only been enough washing powder for one or two wash loads. We arrived back to piles of dirty clothes spewed all over the kitchen floor but no-one had any cash to buy washing powder, as if they would have spent money on that!! We also returned with two weeks of dirty clothes ourselves. What a nightmare.

And I don't know what happened while we were away but the kitchen floor was really sticky. The first job my husband had to do was to attempt to mop the floor, just what you want at 2am. All I wanted was a cup of tea. Not a drop of milk or a single piece of bread to be found. I went to bed.

CHAPTER 16

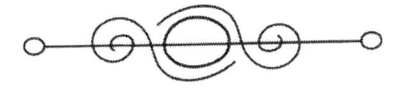

You might be wondering at this point why I felt I needed to separate from my husband. Well I suppose it had been a thirty-year build up, really, of frustrations and irritations. I have to say that my husband is not the man he was – by that I mean he has mellowed considerably – partly due to age and partly due to the fact that he is now retired and a lot of pressure has been lifted off him, and probably partly due to the fact that he doesn't have to live with me anymore. But back in the day I have to tell you he wasn't always an easy man to live with. When you do split up everyone assumes that there has been some major trigger for you that made you leave, but there isn't and there wasn't. Mostly for me anyway it was more a gradual piling up of little stones and when the mound becomes so high you just feel full and don't want to live with it any more.

Very early on in our marriage my husband discovered he was allergic to virtually every food known to man. Many months of research on his part involving keeping food diaries and food testing followed. The upshot of this laborious research took its toll on us both really. For many years of our marriage my husband would prepare his own food and eat separately from the rest of the family. He eliminated all dairy food, rice, potatoes, fruit, tea and coffee and many other things from his diet. Eating together and having a cuppa is quite a bonding process so when you take that out of your lives a major part of that bonding process has gone. My husband was also of the opinion that there was only ever one way of doing things and that was his way. He had the ultimate say in any decisions and choices that were made to do with all thing domestic. Eventually and over many years I felt totally disempowered and insignificant with low self-esteem. Obviously, there had been many occasions and traumas over the years to illustrate how our situation came about, some of which I might talk about later but there was one incident in 2007 when I absolutely knew I'd had enough and we were done.

I had wanted to paint our bathroom. I thought a lovely poppy red would look great with the white suite and tiles so I mentioned it to my husband. I don't recall that he even considered what I'd said apart from probably thinking 'let her talk'. As I'd mentioned it, and there was no obvious opposition I got started one day and when he arrived home from work my mission was complete. A gorgeous red bathroom. He hated it. During the next week or so whenever I went into the bathroom I said how much I loved it and whenever he went in he commented on how dark it was. I then went to visit a friend of mine for a few days and when I arrived back home he'd re-painted my lovely poppy red bathroom. Maybe you have to be a woman to fully appreciate how I felt but I was absolutely furious and more than that, I was really saddened by the fact that something that meant so much to me meant so little to him. He knew I was upset and said he would change it. So the bathroom went from a vile stomach bile yellow to peach and then to white and that's how it stayed. Going back to red was never an option. He asked me what I thought about it and my friend said I should have taken my red paint and written 'fuck you' across the wall. But the damage had been done and I realised I was fighting a losing battle and I would always be a second-rate citizen in that house. He never heard what I said and my feelings counted for nothing and I couldn't really move on from that so that's when I took the decision to move out for a while so we could both do some thinking and consider our positions.

Now I must tell you at this point that I am the kind of person who likes things to be 'proper'. I like the right tools for the job. For example, if you serve pasta I like to use a spoon for serving pasta and if I have a glass of wine I want to have it in a wine glass and not a tumbler! My husband on the other hand was a great believer in 'making do' and 'patching things up'. Not a good combination I'm sure you'll agree. Well there was this one time he'd made a hole in the wall between our kitchen and utility room – something to do with pipework when our washer was re-located. Anyway we ended up with this hole in the wall which looked dreadful... and was also quite draughty! When I mentioned it to him, he sorted it out by stuffing the hole with newspaper. I wasn't happy about this finished product and mentioned it on numerous occasions over the next few years! Eventually when I couldn't stand it any longer and finally exploded, he took out the newspaper and stuffed the hole with socks. Job done. So he could now 'shamfer' things up in his house 'til his heart's content, and I could have things done properly in mine. It worked so much better.

CHAPTER 17

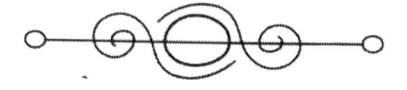

I remember vividly when our first child was born, well every mother would I know, and any subsequent children too for that matter. But it was a little unusual in that my baby girl decided to enter this world two months early. I had only just stopped work the previous week and was anticipating a few weeks of preparation and relaxing before the main event. I had a few weeks (or so I thought) to get all the necessary baby equipment and go to antenatal classes to learn how it was all done. We had been into the city, my husband and me, looking for a pram when I started to feel a bit off really and I had an overwhelming desire to lay down. Not wanting to go home, as the pram mission hadn't been completed, we stopped for a sit down in a café for me to recover. I didn't even want any cake, which was highly unusual! I went to the loo and tried to lay down as flat as I could on the toilet. I remember being aware that there was a gap both above and below the toilet door so I felt quite safe that someone could get to me if necessary. When I finally emerged from the ladies feeling no better, my husband insisted that we go home. The remainder of that Saturday and all through Sunday I didn't feel right. At about 7pm the doctor was called as I kept getting really bad stomach pains, so much so that I had put on some pop socks so there was nothing on my stomach. Do you remember them? Tights material but only went to your knees, usually worn under trousers and looked absolutely hideous. The doctor stood in the doorway as I laid on the sofa and said I must have a kidney infection and promptly left the building. I was a bit concerned actually as I thought a kidney infection when you're seven months pregnant might not be a good thing.

A couple of hours later, and not feeling any better, our cat jumped onto my very large stomach and I felt a warm splurge of liquid run down my legs. My waters had broken. My husband rang 999 and the ambulance duly arrived. As that point I still didn't realise I was about to give birth and thought it was something to do with the kidney infection. (As I said, my antenatal classes hadn't started yet!!) I had to walk to the ambulance down our steep uneven drive aided only by my husband as the ambulance men had shot off and were already back in their vehicle waiting for us. By now I'm starting to struggle. I've got these severe pains in my stomach that seem to reach a peak and then subside – I know I know – how naïve am I? Well the ambulance man wants me to sit down – SIT!! Are you having a laugh? I need to lie down. So I lie down in the back of the ambulance and this guy, smelling strongly of alcohol I have to say, gives me a tube to hold. There should have been a mask at the end of the tube but that had fallen off and this guy is on all fours in the ambulance trying to locate it. Meanwhile I'm feeling really anxious, these pains are becoming really strong and very regular and I'm holding a tube and I don't quite know what I'm expected to do with it. I can't imagine sticking it anywhere is going to help. My husband was really agitated and is telling me to breathe – this wasn't really useful as I had no intention of stopping breathing and found it a bit irritating actually. Meanwhile the ambulance man has retrieved the mask, put it onto the end of the tube I'm still holding and gives it to me to put over my mouth and nose. I took one whiff and felt nauseous so he promptly packed it away. That was his sole contribution to the events. I think he was a bit bored actually and was eager to get back to the pub. I really didn't feel I was getting his full attention! The pub I believe was called 'The Cemetery' and was situated right outside the hospital. A tad insensitive I'd say, but apparently that's where the ambulance men would while away the hours until called out. I think the plug was pulled on that one and the pub's name was changed to something like 'The Florence Nightingale'. I little more uplifting I think.

We eventually arrived at the hospital, having had a sight-seeing tour of Leeds, I swear they didn't take the shortest route but I was in no mood to argue this at the time. I was put in a wheelchair, not comfortable… I needed a stretcher, where was my stretcher? I was taken up to the labour ward and I remember one midwife saying to her colleague that my membrane had ruptured (obviously due to my kidney infection) and I'm wearing pop socks!! Twelve minutes later my baby daughter was born weighing three-and-a-half pounds. I remember the nursing staff kept coming up to me throughout the next few days and saying how quick I was and that I could come again. I did. Three more times.

CHAPTER 18

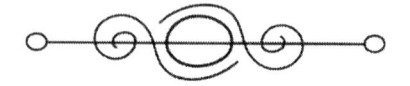

You know, I used to imagine that when you reached middle-age that you had it all 'sussed' and that your life would be sorted and you just sailed along on the calm sea of life – not so, I discovered, of course. Who famously said that life was like a box of chocolates – you never knew what you'd get? Oh yes, Forrest Gump's mum. Well I think life is more like running the Grand National. You go along the flat for a while, everything running smoothly then you come up against an obstacle. You climb over it. Sometimes the 'jumps' are small and you easily get over them sometimes they are quite high and you struggle over it and sometimes you get a 'Becher's Brook' and you think, I can't get over this one, but you grit your teeth and you brace yourself and you do get over it. It leaves you exhausted and weak for a time but you do get over it, and you emerge stronger at the other side and you continue the race. I've had a few Becher's Brooks in my time and will probably have a few more before I shed this mortal coil, but you know, that's just what life is. I never feel surprised or disappointed when things get difficult in my life. It's all part of living and whatever comes your way you just deal with it and move on, it's all part of the journey. I'm lucky in that I never worry about what the future holds, obviously I get concerned and anxious at times if things are seemingly getting difficult for one reason or another, but I don't worry about things unduly. I just wait and see how things unfold and do whatever is necessary at the time. I expect life to get tough at times, so I don't particularly stress about it when it happens.

I remember when my kids were all teenagers and making choices about their futures. I was initially concerned that they were choosing paths for themselves that I maybe hadn't planned for them. I spoke to a cousin of mine about it and he asked me what gave me the right to choose their paths and to have pre-conceived ideas about their futures. I've never forgot what he said and I fully agree with him. I only have the right to choose my own path and they must choose theirs. I can offer advice, of course, I do, but ultimately they make their own decisions and rightly so. If things work out well, great, if not we sort it out and move on. It's their Grand National and I can't run their race. I can perhaps help them climb back on the horse if they stumble and fall off and they continue their race.

CHAPTER 19

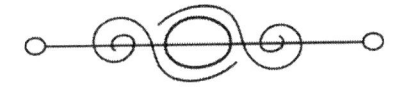

I first met my husband when I was still at school. I was fifteen. He was studying at Leeds University - my home city - and me and a friend would often go to the dances and gigs at the uni. My friend was gorgeous, tall and willowy with a recklessness that was sometimes a bit unnerving. She could always have her pick of the fellas and I usually got the other one. On this particular evening, two students started walking in our direction and I really fancied the one with the long hair. I pleaded with my friend to let me have him – she wasn't interested in either of them especially so she didn't object. Me and my future husband went out together for almost two years. We often stayed in his flat listening to Leonard Cohen and Bob Dylan, which I loved. When I heard Leonard Cohen had died it brought all those old memories back of sitting in that smoky flat listening to him. Our relationship ended quite unexpectedly and we didn't see or hear from each other again for another seven years.

I worked in an office in one of the large department stores in Leeds at the time of our break-up. He would often meet me after work at the staff entrance. Another office worker would often see him waiting for me after work and told me how she would like to go to bed with my boyfriend! Being quite naive at that time I would tell all this to my boyfriend. This girl, who I found rather common and not my type at all, would often join me at break and lunch times in the staff canteen and tell me all about her lurid sex life. I, of course, would repeat all of this to my boyfriend. One day this girl pleaded with me to meet her one evening as she had no single friends to go out with. I reluctantly agreed, truth be told, I found her a bit scary. I told her that I should be meeting my boyfriend that night at the student union bar, but that he wouldn't mind.

As it happened that evening the rain came down with a vengeance and I was thankful to be able to ring her and cancel our night out. Instead I went to my usual haunt, a local disco-come-youth-club and a friend of mine took me down in his car to meet my boyfriend. On arriving there, the first person I saw was this co-office worker I was supposed to have met that night. I was absolutely furious and charged over to my boyfriend who was at the bar with a group of friends. Seven years later I learned that he had no knowledge at that point of her being there. I am shouting like a lunatic, thinking that he knew she was there and that he was interested in her, he's embarrassed in front of his friends, particularly as they are all at university and I'm five years their junior and not at uni – then she comes over crying and saying that she doesn't know what she's done. My boyfriend then decides to comfort her and escorts her back to his flat, and that's how history is made and lives are changed.

I was heartbroken and devastated and incredulous.

He met me at work the next day and said nothing had happened between them, but an older more experienced member of staff told me not to be naive and that if nothing had happened he would have parted company with her where I could have seen. So that was that – he followed me on to my bus home but I was done. She didn't come in to work the next few days and I left that job at the end of the week.

As I said, I never saw or heard another thing from

either of them… oh… apart from one anonymous phone call from one of her friends warning me to stay away from him as he was with her now 'you dirty Jew'.

I did bump into her some years later, (thankfully I was with a very attractive boyfriend at the time) whilst in the city, strangely enough, in the department store we both used to work in, and she told me she had married my boyfriend and that they had a son. I was truly upset as I felt he had been trapped by this girl who clearly had her sights firmly set on having him.

So, life moved on, I had lots of experiences over the next few years, some good, some not so good, but all part of the tapestry of life. All a learning process. Then unexpectedly one evening just before midnight I answered the house phone, we'd moved house but kept the same phone number, and it was him, my old boyfriend. It was very unsettling and I told him I knew he was married and not to contact me again. But call he did and said he wanted us to meet up. I did meet up with him, although I had arranged to meet a friend an hour later, and only because he said if I didn't he knew where I lived and would call round to the house. It was great meeting him actually as he told me how unhappy he was and that it all was a huge mistake, and I was able to say I didn't care and walked away. During our brief meeting, however, there was a fruit machine in the pub where we met which was owned by the company I worked for which I happened to mention, and the firm's details were on the machine.

From then on I kept getting calls from my office saying he'd been ringing them and it had to stop. I agreed to meet him again to tell him to stop ringing my work place as it was starting to cause me a problem, but he told me that he and his wife had separated, that I had always been the love of his life, and would I go out with him, which I then did. And that's how we got back together and eventually got married and had four children together.

CHAPTER 20

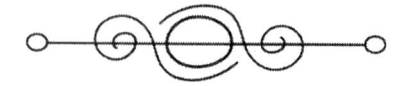

I joined a dating agency at one time on the internet. Well I should say this wasn't something I really had any desire to do as I didn't feel the need to have a man in my life, still don't truth be told, but my estranged husband seemed to be meeting various women and my daughter and me were intrigued as to how this was happening so assumed, correctly as it turned out, that he was 'surfing the net', and decided to try and see where he was and what he had put on about himself. Clearly this was not a simple task as we soon realised there were numerous sites one could join. In order to 'search' I had to register myself onto the site. I was extremely nervous but it was also quite exciting so went along with it. I didn't find my husband initially but by merely registering I found several men were 'winking' at me and making contact. If you've never been on a dating site I suggest you do. I have never known anything quite like it. I have learned a lot. Firstly, most people on there seem only to want to have sex chats! That's been my experience anyway. Now I don't know if I'm just picky but I haven't actually come across anyone I have found to be just normal. I know lots of women through my work and a lot of them are on dating sites and yes they have met up with a variety of men. Not me. Maybe it's me. I was contacted by one man who suggested we might meet up for a coffee, but he couldn't promise he wouldn't be tempted to pour it over my head! I prefer my cappuccino in a cup so declined his offer. Then there was the man whom I'd been talking to for some time but on every occasion we planned to meet either he or a family member had an accident and we had to postpone the meeting. Clearly, he just wanted to chat and never wanted to actually meet up in person. Bizarre. I've been contacted by men from Australia, the US, Norway, Italy and Alaska!! What is the point? Where are you ever going to meet for a coffee? In the middle of the Atlantic!! It's all quite ridiculous really. Having said that it is rather addictive and compelling in its own way and a source of great fun if you take it for what it is and don't have any expectations at all. It is also a great way to spend an evening if there's nothing on the box or if you have a friend round and have a bottle of wine and fancy having some fun. I was once contacted by a fella of 80!! Now I'm not ageist, but 80!! Although I was impressed by his computer skills. I have also been approached by guys as young as 19!! For goodness sake. I tell them not to be so ridiculous and to find a nice girl around their own age. I was approached one time by a man whose English was clearly not up to much and when I queried this he told me he was Italian. He sent me a lovely photo of himself which seemed too good to be true (it was). He was very keen right from the start and sent me pages of poetry which I think must have been taken straight from a book. He declared his undying love for me and said I was his soulmate – all clearly ridiculous – but I wondered where it would all lead so went along with it. It eventually led to him asking me for £2,000. His feelings for me seemed to come to an abrupt end when I told him to find another 'sucker'. Ah... the end of an almost beautiful relationship. Such is life. My membership expired alas, but I might re-join when the long winter nights draw in… it's good to talk… and you never know!

CHAPTER 21

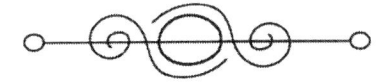

My eldest daughter came back to the UK after about two-and-a-half years travelling abroad. She had lived in Australia and New Zealand for a time and called at numerous other places en-route. When she arrived back home she couldn't settle and moved to Bournemouth with her brother. They had always been close, as had all my kids, and they started work in the licensed trade as a management couple in various public houses. Whilst this suited my son perfectly well my daughter didn't feel comfortable with customers who'd had too much alcohol and took a job managing a coffee shop which suited her much better. She had hated the end of night ritual of trying to get sometimes unwilling customers to leave the premises. My son had no problem with that side of the job and I think actually rather enjoyed it. He's never been shy of confrontation, it's fair to say, when and if necessary.

It was whilst working in a seafront coffee shop my daughter met her husband-to-be. They met in the June and were married six months later on New Year's Eve at Gretna Green. We welcomed him into our family like a breath of fresh air. He was charismatic and full of enthusiasm and as such brought light and colour into our world. What we didn't realise at the time was what we'd thought was enthusiasm and energy was in fact manic behaviour which escalated until three years later he had a complete mental breakdown.

My eldest daughter and her 'to-be' husband left Bournemouth and came back to live in her home town of Sheffield. They both love the sea and didn't want to leave Bournemouth but my youngest daughter who was nineteen at the time was having some problems and had lost her way somewhat. She'd left school before taking her A level exams and started working in a local pub. Her behaviour seemed to be changing, and not for the better. We eventually found out that she had been mixing with what we considered to be undesirable people and had been dabbling with drugs. My eldest daughter felt it might be helpful if she was nearer and to be around for her youngest sister, so they relocated back to Sheffield.

We managed to get my youngest daughter on to a hairdressing course at college and under the tutelage of my now son-in-law, who is a fantastic ladies hairdresser I must say, she gained her hairdressing qualifications. She worked with my son-in-law at a couple of different salons until he opened his own business where she also went to work alongside him. This sounds like there's going to be a happy ending… alas no. As I said my son-in-law's behaviour was becoming more and more grandiose as he hurtled towards a total breakdown.

In January of 2005 my eldest daughter and her husband (married New Year's Eve 2003) had just moved into their first home together after having been in rental properties previously. He had just opened his hairdressing salon and they were expecting their first baby. All very exciting… on the up! My son-in-law's behaviour began to show signs which were starting to be a bit off the wall. He would buy expensive gadgets with no real use for them, be full of nervous energy and jump from project to project. Like the time he decided to go into landscape gardening, bought a £4,000 digger and almost demolished a client's house as well as almost taking out a quarter of the electricity in a local Sheffield suburb. My daughter had no knowledge of their financial situation and he was very secretive and reluctant to discuss it when she tried to find out what was going on.

It was also during this landscaping phase that he bought a trailer in order to collect dozens of sleepers from out of town. My youngest son, recently returned from travelling, accompanied him to get the sleepers, but told him that there was no way the trailer they were using would be able to cope with the weight of the numerous sleepers. My son-in-law, undeterred, loaded up the trailer and began the return journey to Sheffield. Unfortunately, my son was proved right and the trailer wheels started to buckle and finally collapsed under the weight of their load on a busy roundabout. The police duly arrived on the scene amid this chaos and impounded the sleepers which my son-in-law then had to pay a large amount of money to reclaim.

It was soon after this disastrous landscaping attempt that my son-in-law disappeared and couldn't be contacted. My daughter was obviously very concerned as his behaviour had become more and more bizarre. She eventually managed to make contact with him. Unfortunately, he didn't seem to know where he was and so she told him to just get in a taxi and return home. He did, and it turned out he had been at Manchester airport intending to fly to Australia, a country he had travelled to often during his years as a single fella and where he had been born. He had taken a bag with him, which held only a pair of shoes, a book and some underwear. She called the mental health crisis team. Then there was just the small matter of retrieving his abandoned vehicle which was somewhere in the Manchester airport car park! Her dad had to drive over and search for it and then get the AA to break into it so it could be brought back home. The AA took some convincing that this was all legit!!

My son-in-law was subsequently diagnosed as bipolar and the long road to stabilising his condition began. My daughter was very patient and caring and tried her hardest to support him through this difficult period of his life. She tried to encourage him to return to the 'normal' world and one time sent him to the local shop to buy some onions. He returned some four hours later with an onion in one pocket and a block of cheese in the other. After a while my daughter suggested he move out temporarily as it wasn't a suitable environment for their young daughter as his behaviour was erratic and unpredictable. She found him a small cottage nearby to where they lived and continued to buy him food and generally look after him, albeit from a slight distance. He had virtually stopped speaking at all at this point and it was a very difficult time. It was also around this time that the full extent of his money difficulties began to emerge and thing went from bad to worse, culminating in my daughter moving back in with us. This was just before the May Bank holiday weekend.

It emerged that suppliers had been chasing him for some time for bills relating to his business that had not been paid… at all… ever! He had no choice but to be declared bankrupt which meant my daughter had to go into voluntary bankruptcy as all his debts were also hers as his spouse. This was just before their daughter's second birthday. In fact it was the May 2007 bank holiday weekend that me and my husband had rented an apartment in Spain for a little weekend relaxing break. It was also at this time that my youngest daughter found out that she was pregnant and cancelled a planned trip to New York and instead was coming with us and her partner to Spain, the guy she'd been texting all through our Paris trip. My youngest son had recently returned from his world travels. Chaos or what!

My eldest daughter was distraught and moved in with us, my son, just back from travelling, didn't know what the hell was going on and my son-in-law had moved out of the matrimonial home and no-one knew where he was... and we were packing to go away the following day. I was in a total dilemma as I didn't want to leave with my daughter so distressed yet I didn't want to let my other daughter down by cancelling the trip. My recently returned son said to go as he'd be there to 'hold the fort' and comfort his sister. At that time, although we didn't know what my son-in-law's living arrangements were he assured us he would be at the salon that weekend and do his work as usual.

Three weeks earlier me and my husband had effectively bought the business from my son-in-law so we could take over the running of it and relieve him of some of the stress. Too late, unfortunately. We hadn't been fully aware of how bad thing were, and had just injected £10,000 into a black hole.

So me, my husband, my daughter and her partner set off on our 'relaxing' break with very mixed feelings.

We arrived at our holiday apartment which wasn't

really suitable for four adults, although it was advertised as such, and it was very basic. No matter, we were away, time to relax and get a bit of sun. My mobile phone rang first thing the next morning. It was my son. My son-in-law hadn't arrived to open up the salon as promised and there were customers and staff waiting outside - one poor unfortunate woman had been dropped off by her husband as she was on crutches with a leg in plaster, and wasn't due to be collected until some two to three hours later (she was having a colour!).

My son had to scurry down to the salon and open up and try to cancel or re-arrange clients - completely out of his comfort zone! One of the staff members was a lovely young man from Portugal whose command of the English language was not brilliant. He tried his best under the circumstances but as he also couldn't read English too well either, one poor lady who'd gone in for a blonde root touch-up, went out a raging red head. She wasn't too pleased. What a nightmare it all was, and I was once again constantly on my mobile phone trying to organise things from afar. It seemed a very long weekend.

CHAPTER 22

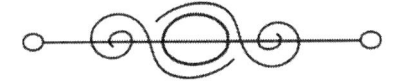

Every parent will have many humorous anecdotes to tell about their kids throughout the years, but there are one or two more memorable ones that stand out for me with my kids.

I remember there was one time I went to put some underwear away for one of my boys in his chest of drawers. I pulled open the drawer to find there was in fact no drawers left – only the fronts. My son had taken out all the insides, lined it with tin foil, placed a lamp inside and was seemingly trying to grow what looked suspiciously like a cannabis plant. All well and good but where were the socks and pants going to go? Then there was the time I awoke one morning to find a rather large polystyrene polar bear and seal cub in my hallway. Goodness only knows here they had come from.

We all, as parents, think we know our kids really well and that they tell us everything. Obviously they don't. I remember finding out long after the event that one of my daughters, who incidentally achieved really good grades at her 'A' levels, had actually missed school on a regular basis and went to listen to quite inappropriate music in some high rise building with a group of significantly older people. Scary or what!

CHAPTER 23

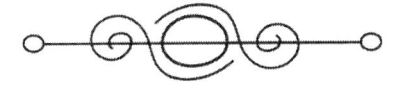

It was a couple of months before my eldest daughter got married that my eldest son met his partner. He was still working in the licensed trade but as a single free male he was sent all over the place. His job was to go into failing pubs to manage and turn them around. It was while working in Cardiff that he met a girl who worked there who he liked very much. She had a boyfriend at the time, but they would have long meaningful chats into the wee small hours. When my son was then sent to run a pub in Birmingham after two weeks, she ditched her boyfriend of two years and joined him. She seemed a lovely girl, very attractive and effervescent. However, when they came to visit us in Sheffield, she would never eat with us and had meals in the loft bedroom they stayed in. I knew this was very strange behaviour but my son tried to convince us (and maybe himself) that she was just extremely shy.

This was a young woman of about twenty-four at the time, she'd been to university and got a degree and worked in the hospitality industry. To suggest that she was that shy was quite ridiculous really. But on subsequent visits she still ate upstairs alone and the distinct smell of cannabis coming from above was quite obvious. It was a difficult time for us as a family as we had to be very careful what we could say to my son as he was by now truly in love with this woman and would not have welcomed any criticism of her. After just four months of being together she became pregnant and their fate was sealed. He decided to leave the licensed trade as he didn't want to work evenings, weekends and holidays with a family or bring up a family on licensed premises. So he gave up his job, which also meant his home and his livelihood to move back to Cardiff with her.

They lived at her mother's house for a time while he retrained to become a carpenter. So with no job, no house and no income and a baby on the way he embarked on the next stage of his life. Not ideal. The next few years were at times intolerably hard for them. They lived in a succession of dreadful rental properties, money was ridiculously tight and things were tough. Then child number two came along.

Life didn't get any easier for them, work for my son was intermittent as it so often is in the trade and then his partner became pregnant again. It made me sad to see how difficult his life was but there are consequences to the choices you make and this was never going to be an easy ride. In addition to having three small boys, irregular work and all the stresses and strains associated with that, my son's partner was proving not to be a very able mother or homemaker. After work my son had to take on a lot of the household tasks and see to the children. I think his partner had her own demons to deal with and took to escaping in alcohol and probably other substances. I'm just thankful that my son is strong and throughout all his difficulties it hasn't changed his basic personality. Even in the face of some extremely difficult times which have almost broken him, he has remained the person he always was. He hasn't become bitter or resentful or ever felt sorry for himself. He's remained resilient, strong and kept his basic enthusiasm intact.

CHAPTER 24

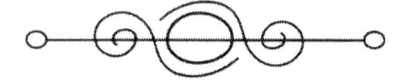

My kids find it amusing that something always seems to happen to me when I go on holiday. It invariably starts at the airport when I always 'bleep' when I try to go through the security scanner. After the usual patting me up and down and without having to ever endure any further, more intimate, investigation I am always allowed through. Thankfully. That said and with them now being adults with families of their own, it appears my 'holiday gene' might have been passed down the generations.

On one occasion, well it didn't fall into the category of holiday exactly, but a day trip my son took with his partner and three children, they had a disturbing and unusual experience. They had decided to go to a safari park. The kids were understandably very excited to be seeing animals at such close range. They'd driven through the usual places, monkeys, lions, rhinos etc and then at last they came to an area where they could buy some animal food, open the windows and feed the reindeer. All seemed ok at first, there were a few reindeer dotted about, none of them particularly interested in the food that was being offered but enjoyable for the kids nevertheless, eagerly trying to entice them over with a few pellets of reindeer food.

Then seemingly out of nowhere, a rather large adolescent male reindeer with huge antlers started towards their vehicle. Assuming all was well, as this was a safe area to feed the animals, they didn't feel unduly alarmed as this large reindeer approached them. As soon as this beast was alongside them he started headbutting their vehicle. The kids were screaming and the adults started to frantically close the car windows. My son, who was driving, had no way of escape as there were cars both in front and behind them. He tried to manoeuvre the car in the limited space available but the beast was seriously attracted to their vehicle and followed them, headbutting and making deep indentations in the car all down the left side from front to back bumper.

Amid the din of screams, hysteria and car horns honking, they eventually managed to make their escape. The safari park management were full of apologies and agreed to pay for the vehicle to be repaired. They also gave them free tickets for a return visit but the children were by now too traumatised to want to repeat the experience.

They've never been keen on visiting Santa either come to think of it – I guess they just don't want to see the reindeer!!

CHAPTER 25

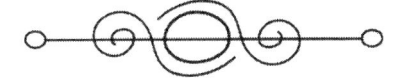

So, after thirty years of being together me and my husband had a parting of the ways and moved into our own separate new homes. We planned to stay married as there didn't seem any need to change that. But as my sixtieth birthday approached and after being married for thirty-six years, there was the little matter of my portion of his pension to sort out.

Me and my husband couldn't agree on the amount with regard to the percentage of his pension that I was due. He thought I should receive significantly less than I felt I was entitled to after such a long marriage. Unfortunately, at that stage, solicitors had to be involved and I felt it was perhaps time we actually got divorced and made it a more solid arrangement. It was a difficult time for us both and there was a lot of unpleasantness and upset. It's strange how being fair is dependent on which window you are looking out of. After hundreds of pounds being spent in solicitor's fees an agreement was reached which we both felt we could live with. But damage had been done and things had soured between us and we didn't communicate for many weeks. All very sad, and all over money. Our divorce was made absolute on Friday 13th December 2013. In February 2014, two months later, I received a surprise phone call from my now ex-husband saying that he had been diagnosed with terminal cancer. I was absolutely devastated. Our friendship resumed and we spent a lot of time together in the following six months leading up to his passing in the August of that year.

Three weeks after my husband's (sorry ex) diagnosis my youngest daughter rang me from hospital to say she'd been diagnosed with cancer. It was the one single most terrible day of my life. She'd had gynaecological problems for over a year and eventually when everything the GP had tried wasn't resolving the problem she was referred to the hospital for more comprehensive investigations. Needless to say the next few weeks were hellish. The wait between hospital appointments was torturous. But eventually she was told that she had fibroids and that a medical procedure would resolve the problem. She duly had the procedure and we rejoiced - this was short-lived unfortunately as when she went back to the hospital for her post-operative examination she was informed that she actually had cervical cancer. This was just before her thirtieth birthday.

My daughter, whose children were then aged three and six, wasn't living with her husband at that time. He'd been irresponsible with money and she couldn't tolerate the numerous phone calls, letters and people coming to the door demanding payment for one thing or another, so they had separated. After my daughter's surgery she came with the children to live with me to recuperate. To be fair, her husband, who has always been and still is a good dad, stepped up to the mark and did everything he could to be supportive. Their relationship improved and after she was well enough they resumed living back together again.

At this time my ex-husband's health hadn't appeared to deteriorate and we continued going out together for lunches, evening meals and visits to see our children and grandchildren etc. By the July of that year he was getting more tired but that was the only sign that he wasn't his usual self. A palliative nurse came to see him about that time and asked if he had or wanted to know how long he might have left. He didn't. He said he knew it was probably only months, not years. As she was leaving, she beckoned me to the door and told me it was weeks rather than months. I just couldn't believe it, he seemed so well. From then on, however, he did deteriorate quite quickly. He grew more and more tired and started to lose weight at an alarming rate. In a very short time after that he couldn't manage the stairs and a hospital bed was brought in. I moved in to live with him about that time. He had said he wanted to remain at home until the end and I promised him that he would.

The last few weeks we spent together were quite lovely. It felt like it was just me and him just like it had been in the beginning, before children and grandkids. I think we both felt we had come full circle. We were once again very close. I felt it was an absolute privilege to be the person he wanted there with him at the end and that all our differences and misunderstandings over the years just melted away.

The last couple of weeks before he died were very difficult, both emotionally and physically. He had become very weak and couldn't get to the bathroom or eat and drink without a lot of assistance. My daughters were wonderful and stayed with us as much as they could, but as his health deteriorated I started to feel I was way out of my depth with the care and assistance I could give him. But I wasn't going to let him go into a hospice as his wish was to remain in his own home until the end. I was in turmoil, as I knew he needed more help that I was equipped to give. The final straw came when one Saturday night I was trying to support him in getting to the bathroom and he fell backwards, full length on the kitchen floor. Thankfully my eldest daughter was sleeping over and I shouted her downstairs in complete panic to help me try to get her dad back up. It was a most dreadful time and I wanted and needed to get some expert help, but was still anxious that if we called for some assistance and if it was seen we weren't managing, that the decision to stay at home would be taken away from us and I couldn't allow that to happen. I didn't know what to do for the best.

That very next morning, amazingly, a good friend of mine rang me to see how we were all coping. She is very high up in the administration of our local hospice. I broke down and told her of the trauma of the previous night. She immediately assured me that a care package could be provided in the home and contacted the relevant people to put a care plan in place. From then on until he passed away we had nurses visiting throughout the day to clean and change him and make him comfortable in a way I clearly could never have done. We didn't need night care as I slept downstairs opposite him and watched him throughout the night. We knew the end was very close and contacted his son from his first marriage who lived in Australia. He organised to fly over immediately and was with him at the end as we all were. He finally passed away on a beautiful sunny day on Sunday 31st August 2014.

CHAPTER 26

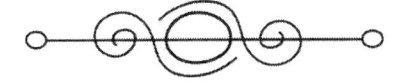

It was just prior to both my husband's and daughter's diagnoses that my salon was burgled. It was almost unbelievable actually. I am a great believer in following rules and am always on the ball with paying bills and insurances etc, but at that precise time the insurance cover for my salon was drawing to an end and I had decided to change to another company which gave me a more suitable and comprehensive cover for my needs. Although I was in the process of taking out my new cover a good two weeks in advance of my old cover expiring, I needed to sign a hard copy of the new policy. The company I had decided to use was sending me out the relevant document in the post for me to sign and return to them. As luck would have it when I received their letter in the post the document I needed to sign hadn't been enclosed. I rang them to tell them that the enclosure had been omitted. They apologised and said they would forward me another which they duly did but it delayed the whole process for a further week or so. The unfortunate delay meant that for three days I had no insurance cover for my salon. In almost twenty years of having my business I have only been without insurance cover for three days… and that is when my salon was burgled. Only the office was targeted so we were still able to continue to work thankfully. But it was a ball ache and took my daughter many hours to reinput all the paperwork onto a new computer, when we managed to get one, ready to give to the accountant.

The girls had also been saving money which I kept for them in the office and I felt it my responsibility to reimburse them over the next few weeks. Unbelievably, I had done the girls' wages on the Wednesday evening instead of my usual Thursday morning and had taken them home with me, along with money and cheques for paying into the bank, which was almost unprecedented. I paced the floor over the next couple of nights and laid awake in bed not being able to absorb the unfortunate timing of the burglary, but all that paled into insignificance when both my husband and daughter dropped their bombshells. Everything is relative and I have tried to train myself not to stress about things that I have no control over. Not always easy.

CHAPTER 27

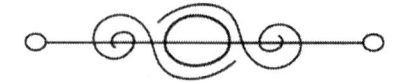

Have I ever mentioned how absolutely diabolical my sense of direction is? Well that's not strictly true. Put me on a motorway… no problem. I can travel north to south, east to west, all perfectly fine. I can also probably name most of the service stations along the way too, but get me three or four minutes away from my final destination and I'm struggling. I just seem to totally lose my bearings in the last few minutes of my journey, even though I'm then often on familiar territory, so to speak. Bizarre really. I just seem to get disorientated in the very final stages of a journey. I find it particularly difficult getting out of car parks and out of supermarket service stations. Anyone who is with me thinks I'm just messing about

- but I really am not.

Bearing this in mind, one Sunday my daughter had an hour or so to kill before her brother was due to arrive at her house for a visit with his little girl, and the weather was beautiful. I know, says I... I'd been for a lovely walk the previous week in the countryside with my other daughter. The route we had taken was only thirty or forty minutes long. Perfect. So off we went, me, my daughter, her two young children ... and her very very pregnant dog who was due to deliver her pups in the next five to seven days.

It started so well. I remembered the route we'd previously taken and I am leading the way. After about thirty minutes and nearing the end of our lovely walk, the timing having been perfect as I had said it would be, I must have taken a wrong turn. Had I looked over my right shoulder at about a sixty-degree angle I would have seen the car park and all would have been well. But unfortunately, not so and on we trekked. After another half hour or so and after my daughter had rung her brother to put back his visit a little, I was beginning to realise something wasn't quite as it should be. We took numerous twist and turns to try to get back to our vehicle, each one looking familiar to me, but alas not right. Three hours later, hot, exhausted, unable to speak to me and having had to carry her pregnant dog, who was seriously struggling I must admit by this time, we were re-united with our car and travelled back in total silence. I had asked a pleasant looking gentleman for directions at one stage, but he responded in a very abrupt and rude manner. I wasn't trying that again.

My daughter, along with the children and dog, all stayed over at my house that same night as we had planned a quick shopping trip after having taken the children to school the following morning. We left my home at the usual time, 8.20am, to do the school run then proceeded straight on to the shopping mall. The dog had been perfectly content to remain in her basket in my kitchen (probably recovering from the previous afternoon's walk).

Of course the quick 'in and out' shopping trip took a tad longer than expected and so then a bit of lunch was needed. We arrived back at my house about 1.30 – but unusually the dog didn't run excitedly to greet us. A little alarmed, as this was most unusual, we entered the house with slight trepidation. We searched downstairs calling her name - nothing. We then cautiously went up the stairs. OMG, it looked like a scene from a horror movie. There on my bed were two tiny white puppies. As mummy dog was all black this was strange enough but it was the sight of the blood soaked, previously beautiful all white bed linen that looked so shocking. After waiting a further four hours or so to see if there were to be any more pups, my son-in-law placed the newborn pups in a shoe box and they all went back to their home. I shot down to the nearest suitable shop and bought a new duvet and new white bed linen!

My daughter rang me three hours later to say two more pups had arrived and then another one arrived another hour later! All most unusual.

CHAPTER 28

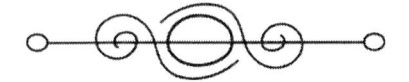

Every year for the last twelve years or so me and a friend of mine have taken time out and treated ourselves to a three night stay in one of the UK's top health farms.

It happened quite accidentally actually. In 2001, me and another good friend of mine started saving money every week in a Post Office account so that when we reached the ripe old age of fifty we would go to New York for a few days to acknowledge that particular milestone. I'd had the idea on a flight back from New Zealand where I'd been to visit my daughter. She had been travelling, supposedly for one year, but after over two years away I decided I couldn't stand it any longer and booked a flight to go see her. Anyway, feeling brave, as travelling to New Zealand was far and away the most exciting and adventurous thing I'd ever done, I came up with the New York idea. After saving for over a year we did go to New York, but more of that later. But on our return we continued to save and each year I used the money to go to a health farm - a luxury I couldn't have splurged out on in one fell swoop, that would have felt too extravagant, but with saving each week I felt I could justify it.

Incidentally, it was on my first or second trip to the Health Farm that I told my friend about the time I had taken out a £10,000 loan for my daughter and her husband, with the intention that they would take it over when their credit rating improved (which they did). Only I hadn't told my husband about this as I knew he wouldn't agree to it, and I thought it would all be sorted without him ever having to worry himself about it. Due to a rather unfortunate incident involving my son-in-law however, my husband did find out and went absolutely berserk. My husband would generally go icily quiet when angry and not shout or carry on, but on this occasion he was unusually vocal and I actually thought he was going to punch a hole in the brick wall. So... I'm telling my friend about this as we head down the motorway and unusually instead of commiserating with me about his strange ways, she actually said she had to agree with him, it was a most unusual occurrence.

People go to health farms for a variety of reasons, some keep fit, engage in various gym classes, swim, walk, run, play tennis etc. Me and my friend do nothing. Absolutely nothing. When we first arrive we change into the standard attire of white towelling robe and slippers and stay like that until we leave three days later. We don't even get dressed to eat dinner – it's great. We do manage to struggle into a cozzie to do the spa rooms and we do get into PJs at night, but other than that, it's robe and slippers all the way! To be fair, for the first ten years or so we both had very busy working lives and the time out at the health farm was the perfect battery recharge, but I can't say either of us have been exactly overworked in the last couple of years, but the habit just continued.

In the early years we often added extra treatments to the ones included in our stay but over the years we haven't even bothered doing that. We've found the inclusive treatments have been sufficient for our needs. It's been more about stepping out of your life for a few days and not being instantly available through Facebook/text/mobile phones etc that has been what has appealed to us.

There was this one occasion when I was waiting to be 'collected' by my therapist from the reception area for my shoulder and back massage, and this tiny, slightly-built little girl called my name and said she'd be my therapist for the treatment. I was a bit surprised as she didn't look like she had the strength to hold the towel never mind doing any sort of meaningful massage. But I lay down on the bed face down as was required. I don't know if she left the room and a sumo wrestler entered via a concealed entrance but my God, the weight she exerted on my back was unbelievable. I kept wanting to turn round and have a peek to see who was doing my massage but I didn't dare. At the end of a gruelling fifty minute treatment the little slightly-built, teeny tiny girl was still there, smiling and asking me if I enjoyed it. Unbelievable.

In the early years of going to the health farm I had decided to book a treatment which I think was some sort of flotation experience. It sounded great actually and conjured up images of relaxing and drifting off somewhere lovely. I anticipated gentle music playing and being surrounded by sweet fragrant air. Wrong. Alarm bells sounded as the 'treatment' was being outlined to me by the therapist. I first had to lather my underarms and private parts with petroleum jelly from a tub with a spatula. I then had to immerse myself in what could only be described in my mind as resembling the underbelly of a submarine, bare walls painted in a bright blue metallic looking paint. I was then supposed to lie there for thirty minutes in total silence (no gentle music) and in total darkness while the therapist sat outside. There was a button I could press to summon the therapist if I felt I couldn't take it any longer or if I had a panic attack I guess. It felt more like total sensory deprivation and not relaxing in any shape or form. I did manage the thirty minutes of this torture… but it wasn't easy, enjoyable or relaxing at all. I did try to talk my friend into sharing this experience on our next visit there but for some reason it had been taken off the menu so to speak. I can't think why!

I have always enjoyed the annual visits to the health farm with my friend. We have always gone in January or February which has been perfect timing for me as December was always a very busy time at the salon working very long days with virtually no days off. The last time we went, though, wasn't quite so good as I was feeling unwell and was coughing almost continually. The coughing irritated the hell out of me so must have driven my poor friend crazy. In addition to the constant coughing I kept having spontaneous nose bleeds, which was most inconvenient, I had about eight throughout our three-day stay.

The last and longest 'bleed' was unfortunate. It was while I was having the usual back and shoulder massage. I was lying on my front with my face in the air hole that beauty couches have (so you don't suffocate) when my nose started to bleed. I didn't want to spoil the moment as the therapist was doing such a good job and we were involved in an interesting conversation but after having bled through the hole for a few seconds and realising it was dripping onto the floor and that it wasn't going to stop any time soon I had to interrupt the proceedings and alert the therapist of the situation. She was kindness personified but I had to abandon the treatment and any further treatments unfortunately. I suppose I was in the best place to be unwell really, lying around all day with nothing to do but relax but it wasn't as enjoyable as it usually was I must say.

In the early years of going to the health farm my friend and I explored all the facilities on offer (apart from the gym!) and we were really looking forward to going into the 'retreat' or quiet room. This was a room that was decorated in lovely flowery wallpaper and looked rather like a room from a bygone age. In this room there was an assortment of different pieces of furniture one could recline and relax on and drift off into one's own thoughts, daydreams or into blissful sleep. There was a four poster bed, swing seats, a chaise lounge, a couple of rather large bean bags etc. The only requirement whilst in this room was SILENCE – so no rattling of a newspaper for example and of course, no chattering. I think it took about four years before we managed to enter this room on our first attempt. It just seemed so absurd and comical. We would open the door and see people all laid out in various positions on the beds and couches and would just always burst out laughing. It would take four or five attempts at deep breathing to calm ourselves down before we could enter.

The 'candle room' unfortunately had the same effect on us too for some reason. This was a room in the spa area where you walked down a few steps and lie on raised beds in the water with subdued lighting that was in the shape of candles. I could never see the point of it really and as I could never lie on the raised bed without floating away, decided to give that a miss on future visits!

CHAPTER 29

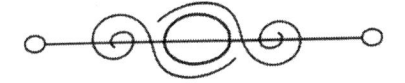

Long before having my own business I worked as a childminder. I did that for thirteen years. It had a number of benefits at the time and fitted in perfectly with where I was in my life. I had my own four young children and wanted to be there for them throughout their childhood. Childminding meant I could be. I could also earn some money at the same time.

There were a few scary moments throughout those thirteen years, as there would be when you have pre-school children for that number of years in your care. Of course there were the usual bumps and bruises children get as part of growing up but there were two incidents which were rather more than that and are indelibly imprinted in my mind.

We had all arrived back at my house from doing the usual school pick-up one day. I had three under-fives that I looked after at the time, along with a further six kids I collected from school that day and with my own four there was a total of thirteen children. Not a problem. They all had drinks and biscuits which was the usual after-school routine, then some of the younger ones played with toys around the house while some of the older ones chose to play outside in our rather large garden with all the usual combinations of swings and slides etc. All of a sudden there was an almighty scream and all hell broke loose. I rushed outside to see my eldest son sat on the ground cradling one of my childminding kids. My son had his hand over this boy's forehead and they were both covered in blood. All the other children were screaming and crying and running around in panic, and although I had completed all my first aid training, I too went into total panic mode and was running round like a headless chicken with one of the younger kids in my arms. Luckily my son, who was also trained in first aid, remained calm and told me to ring for an ambulance.

The boy in question had been running and had tripped. Unluckily, he had fallen head first against a sharp edge on a wall. Blood was pouring from near his eye and my son was applying pressure to stem the flow while speaking calmly to him to try to stop him falling into an unconscious state. The ambulance duly arrived and the boy had to have his head stitched, but thankfully it had just missed his eye. Sometime later my son received a note thanking him for 'saving his life'!

Then there was another occasion, which incidentally made me decide to stop childminding. I felt that maybe after thirteen years the odds of something seriously life-threatening happening to one of my charges were getting shorter. My own children were now of an age where I should move on and look for a job outside the home, in the real world! On this particular day I was looking after two young sisters, one was just over three years old and the other was a baby of about seven months whose mother had not long returned to work after her maternity leave. It was an ordinary day, I had just collected the older girl from toddler group where she had made a lovely fish covered in beads and sequins. I was preparing some lunch and the baby was rolling and crawling around on the carpeted hall where I could keep an eye on her. All of a sudden and totally out of the blue, she seemed to be choking. I rushed to her, grabbed her up in my arms and tried to see what she might have put in her mouth. Nothing. There had been nothing on the floor that was remotely small enough for her to have put in her mouth, just a couple of soft toys and rattles. After a few seconds she seemed to recover. Then suddenly, and as I was still holding her she started choking again. This happened four or five times and each time she was getting more and more distressed – and so was I. I couldn't feel or see anything in her mouth that could be causing the problem and I just couldn't understand what was happening. In desperation, I called her mum, as this was developing into a serious situation. Fortunately the mum worked at the local school and was a first aider. She came down immediately. She also couldn't understand what was happening so decided to take the baby to the hospital for further investigations. Apparently en-route to the hospital, she later told me, the baby stopped breathing completely and mum had to give her mouth-to-mouth resuscitation.

Seemingly what had happened it later transpired was that a sequin that had fallen off her sister's fish had lodged in her windpipe and would lay flat for a time then it would flap up, closing off her airway. Her throat had minor lacerations due to the sharpness of the sequin. It all ended well, thankfully, and mum was still more than ok about the children staying in my care. I continued for a further three weeks until the start of the school summer holidays, but then I was done. My childminding days were over.

I must say though, there had been some really good and fun times throughout those childminding years. In particular there was one winter's day when I'd taken all the kids up to school. It was a cold day and the sky looked to be filled with snow clouds, but we'd made it up the hill to school easily enough and I'd arrived back home without any problem. I was looking after two-year-old twin boys at the time. About midday the snow started to fall and it came down relentlessly for hours. As school pick-up time drew near I didn't have a clue how I'd get up that hill with two little ones who could never have walked through all that snow. Using the car was completely out of the question and the double buggy was also a non-starter.

I rang a good friend of mine who had to pass by my house on her way to school, to see if she had any suggestions. She walked round to mine and we had a think about what to do. She also had her own children to collect plus others that she looked after so one of us staying at mine with the twins wasn't really an option. Then we had a eureka moment! I had some bivi bags in my garage from when my own boys went on camping trips with scouts. We put the twins in the bivi bags and between us hauled them up the snow covered hill to school. It took us ages to get there, mainly because we were laughing so much. The twin boys loved it. We must have been quite fit in those days!

CHAPTER 30

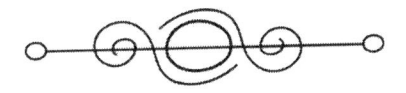

Looking back, we did have some funny times along the way, me and my husband. Well I say funny but probably more embarrassing (and some bloody awful) and probably only funny looking back with hindsight.

Like when my sister-in-law and family were coming to visit us for the day from out of town. My sister-in-law is a lovely lady and in the last few years, largely due to my (ex) husband's illness we've reached a better understanding of each other it's fair to say. But way, way back then I always felt quite inadequate in her company and always felt she was rather disapproving of me. You see, she always seemed very ordered and 'proper' in her life, while in comparison I felt we lived a more chaotic lifestyle. She had lovely matching tableware and tea sets etc while I always seemed to end up with a mishmash of assorted items. Of course, I now realise, none of this matters in the great scheme of things, but when you're younger - much younger - these things held more significance. Anyway the day of the visit. They were of course staying for dinner and I managed to get my kids to put out the knives and forks – no-one mentioned spoons, so why they had been put out goodness only knows. But after the meal was over my poor brother-in-law was toying with his spoon eagerly awaiting dessert. Well there wasn't one. I just hadn't thought of it. My kids usually had a piece of fruit or a yoghurt. To make matters even worse he didn't believe there was no 'afters' and thought I was just joking. Also, my sister-in-law was a fabulous baker and had studied home economics in further education! Her pavlovas could equal anything on *Bake Off*!! We hadn't got off the best of starts either as before dinner my husband had asked who would like a drink and unfortunately, we all said yes, only to find we didn't have enough glasses, someone had to drink their wine out of a mug. Now, of course, none of these things would embarrass me, although I do like things to be right and proper.

Then there was the time me and my husband had been invited to a very posh family do. My husband hired a suit, shoes and the lot, as our lives didn't necessitate having these items. We set off up the M1 motorway for this fabulous evening out. When we arrived there were some beautiful vehicles with private number plates parked outside. I was really looking forward to it but I think my husband was feeling a bit inadequate and out of his comfort zone. Still, there was lovely food and conversation and a chance for me to catch up with long lost family... and a free bar. It's fair to say that my husband drank a lot that night, maybe to give him Dutch courage... I don't know. But on the journey back, as I was driving he was getting more and more agitated and worked up and suddenly started removing his hired clothes and throwing them out of the car window, including the shoes! I was furious and probably driving way too fast and he was left wearing just a pair of trousers by the time we arrived home. I stormed up to bed followed by him moments later, insisting I go back downstairs and shave all his hair off. Seriously not amusing at the time but utterly ridiculous and funny in hindsight. I never did find out how he explained that one to the suit hire company.

There was another occasion when we had all gone

to a lovely Chinese restaurant for one of my daughter's birthdays. My kids were all in their teens at this time and we had all had a fair amount of alcohol (not the designated driver of course), and when we arrived home we all decided to shave our heads, not completely, but very nearly, apart from my youngest daughter who was having none of it and shot upstairs to bed. What is it with us and head shaving? Anyway, I kept that look for a while as I rather liked it, and my husband would periodically shave it for me. But there was this one time he forgot to put the comb on the end of the clippers and did one swipe up the centre of my head which was then completely bald. He felt really bad about it and said he'd blend it in somehow, which was clearly an impossibility. So I had to have it all done the same. People would give my sympathetic looks as it was clear they assumed I was suffering from a really serious illness.

CHAPTER 31

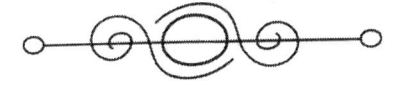

As I mentioned earlier, my 'holiday gene' seems to have been passed down through to the next generation. My youngest daughter had planned a weekend trip to London for her husband's thirtieth birthday. They brought their eleven-month-old daughter to me for the weekend. They also brought her soiled cot bedding as she'd been sick in the night and they didn't have time to sort it out. At this point in time my daughter was absolutely fine and looking forward to some special time together with her partner and seeing a show she had booked.

Unfortunately on the train journey down she started to feel unwell and by the time they arrived at the hotel she'd booked, which incidentally didn't live up to expectations either, and was merely a tiny basic room with a TV, she was feeling really ill. She tried to soldier on and make it to the meal that had been booked, but could only manage a small taste of the soup and had to return to the hotel bedroom where she continued to be sick for the remainder of the weekend. She started to pick up on the return train journey and by the time they arrived back home she was fully recovered.

Their honeymoon hadn't been brilliant either. They'd gone to Corfu but again the room wasn't up to much and the only view from their window was of a wall and the cleaning staff who passed by on a regular basis. Still not to be downhearted they decided to go to a really lovely restaurant for their final evening meal. Unfortunately my daughter got food poisoning and spent the whole trip on the coach back to the airport being sick in her straw sunhat!!

CHAPTER 32

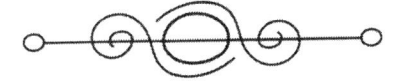

When me and my business partner decided to part company I thought it was a good time to give the salon a makeover. My son-in-law who works in the trades was more than willing to take on the job. I did have one or two reservations about this as although he is extremely good in his particular trade, I wasn't totally convinced he was up to doing a job that had a lot of different components to it. This was based on the fact that he had previously undertaken a couple of jobs outside his remit and had to abandon them prior to completion! Still he seemed quite confident in taking on the challenge and assured me he could call on other tradesmen to help in the areas when and where necessary.

To cut a long story short I should have gone with my gut instinct and not let this situation arise. The whole job turned out to be a bit of a nightmare and ended up costing me far more than anticipated as I had to enlist the help of outside tradesmen to complete the job. Some of whom I know ripped me off. It was all a bit stressful as during all this refurbishment I had a time limit as to how long the salon could be closed for these works to be done. You might have thought I had learned from that experience but alas no – eight years later when I decided to relocate into larger premises my son-in-law once again seemed very confident that he could do the job and offered his services. This was a much bigger project than the previous work as it was spread over three floors of a virtually derelict building and needed everything doing, from re-wiring to laying floors, making partition walls and new ceiling etc.

I should have recalled my dad's words of many years earlier, that to make one mistake is forgivable, but to do it again makes you a fool. And what a fool I was. The estimate my son-in-law had given me was underestimated by at least two thirds. As the deadline for opening was getting ever closer it was clear the new premises were a million miles away from being completed on time. I was in total panic and think it must have reduced my life expectancy by five years at least. I had to eventually take out two additional credit cards and draw on all my contacts to bring workers in to complete the job on time. We eventually finished the work by midnight of the evening before we were due to open the next day. I was so stressed and exhausted I wanted to run away from it all and have nothing more to do with it... ever. Still the salon opened and all went well and it ran beautifully until I sold it five years later.

I must say, I had never planned moving to larger premises. I was fifty-nine at the time and was winding down so to speak. But both my daughters were now involved in the business and the plan was to expand so that in the not too distant future they would take it over and I would bow out to a large extent. This would have all worked out fine. My credit cards were slowly being paid off as was my business loan, but in the October of 2015 I had the bright idea and made the suggestion to both of my daughters that we should all emigrate to New Zealand and have a fresh start.

I should have been content with my life, I owned my own home, I had a thriving business which both my daughters worked in alongside me, we all lived within walking distance of each other... all lovely. But I also had a renewed taste for adventure in view of the dreadful events of 2014. I felt I had been to the jaws of hell and survived and now nothing could touch or particularly scare me now. I felt Teflon coated.

So, in October, having thought about it for a while I sounded out my eldest daughter first, on the prospect of us all starting over at the other side of the world. She had lived in New Zealand for about a year during her travels some fifteen years earlier and had loved the country. I had also visited her there during that time, and loved it too. It didn't feel 'foreign' and everything just seemed so much more tranquil, gentle and spacious.

She immediately thought it was a great idea. She had always had a hankering to live in New Zealand but felt she could never go and leave both me and her sister as we are all very close. We always knew though that perhaps her younger sister might not be so keen on the idea, and it wasn't anything we had ever even discussed at all up until that point. It was a big ask. We also knew that we all went or no-one went, so as attractive and exciting as it seemed, neither of us really thought it would become a reality.

When I say 'all of us' I mean me and my two daughters and their families. One of my sons lived in

Cardiff and the other one was in the military and only spent a couple of years in one place before being relocated. Consequently we didn't see a lot of either of them and their families and as sad as it would be to leave them I felt our leaving the UK would have minimal impact on them and their lives.

The next step was to sound out my youngest daughter. Surprisingly, she didn't think we were crazy and was immediately interested and excited by the prospect of a new start. But she didn't think her husband would even consider leaving the UK, his family and all he had ever known. Unbelievably, when she discussed it with him, he was immediately on board. So that was that.

We then had to do some serious fact finding and see where we went next.

In February of the following year there was an expo being held in Birmingham for people interested in emigrating to New Zealand, Australia and Canada. We booked tickets for the expo and waited. We didn't tell anyone of our plans, as we were so far away from it becoming a reality, if indeed it ever did. I did tell both my sons of course. I spent a weekend with both of them and let them know our intentions. They were both completely shocked and surprised by the news… how could they not be?

February 14th it was – Valentine's Day – and we travelled to Birmingham to find out what was involved and to see if we were even eligible. We knew my eldest daughter wouldn't have a problem getting into New Zealand as her husband had been born in Australia which gave him automatic entry to New Zealand. My other son-in-law found out that with his trade, he could apply to go in as a skilled migrant. New Zealand was really wanting skilled tradesmen from the UK to help with all the re-building work needing to be done because of the 2011 earthquake.

My situation was a little different as my age was against me and I didn't in effect have anything to offer the country. I found out that I couldn't apply for a permanent residency until I had a child who had been a resident there for three years, and then there would be no guarantees I'd get in. So in effect I could visit New Zealand but would have to keep leaving for a few months at a time until I was eligible to visit again. But if that's what it took then that's what I would do.

CHAPTER 33

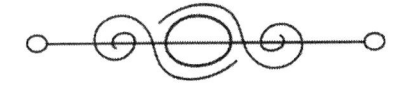

My daughters had both moved into their own homes in 2015. Well, I say their own homes. In actual fact, neither of them could get a mortgage at that time as they were both self-employed and only worked part-time due to them both having small children. Consequently they were both paying huge amounts in rented properties. They had both inherited money, as had their brothers, from their dad who'd passed away the previous year. I, of course didn't inherit, as we'd been divorced eight months earlier. So we decided that they would 'gift' their inheritance to me and I would put it down on a deposit for both on houses for them. They would obviously make the repayments and any other expenses associated with the houses but wouldn't be paying huge, crippling rents with private landlords. So to go forward and speed up the process, the decision was made for me to sell my house, which I owned outright, and in effect 'buy' theirs by giving them the market value at that time and thereby freeing up their money so they could finance their move to New Zealand. This would also give me an income for a few years whilst I was tooing and froing between the UK and New Zealand until I could hopefully get my permanent residency in the fullness of time. At which time I could sell the houses and finance my own resettlement in New Zealand.

My first priority was to come to some arrangement about my salon.

On our return journey from the Birmingham expo, I rang the girl who had worked with me for over sixteen years and arranged to meet her with her husband at a local pub. I needed to let her know of our plans and see if she wanted first refusal on buying the business. She was naturally shocked by our decision to emigrate but said she would give it some consideration. I then put my house up for sale. After careful consideration she decided that she didn't want to buy the business at that stage but we came up with a plan for her to manage it in my absence and if after a couple of years she decided she wanted to take it on more permanently, it would be hers.

After the usual stresses and uncertainties of selling a house the sale went through on 20th June 2016. On the 1st June – my birthday – the international removers arrived at my house, after already having packed up my youngest daughter's house, and packed all my goods and chattels into their van to be shipped across the sea.

The plan was for me to move into my eldest daughter's home until her visa was granted and we would travel together to New Zealand, first stopping en-route in Los Angeles and Fiji. Her husband had secured a job offer in New Zealand and was the first to leave the UK to sort out accommodation etc. My youngest daughter should have been leaving the UK at the beginning of June, also with her husband and children, but because of her medical history there was further medical information required before her visa could be granted. As her husband had already got the offer of a job, he had to leave to take up his new position before her visa was granted. Because of this unforeseen delay for her it meant she and her children had to unexpectedly move in with her sister in the interim as her house had a tenant due to move in on 11th June.

So there we were, three of us adults and four children all living in this sparsely furnished house. My eldest daughter's household contents, apart from a few basics, had also been packed and were being shipped overseas along with mine and her sisters. Not what had been planned exactly but unexpected things happen especially with such a huge undertaking. We managed to muddle through the next six weeks or so, alternating the sleeping arrangements so we all had a turn at sleeping in a bed! My eldest daughter's visa was granted and we were due to leave the UK on 14th July, arriving one week later in New Zealand to coincide with all our house contents arriving on 22nd July. The only problem was that my youngest daughter's visa still had not been granted by this point and the additional information immigration required was proving to be a lengthy process. In fact there was still uncertainty as to whether it would be granted at all.

It was with heavy hearts me, my daughter and her children left on 14th July, we were leaving my youngest daughter in her sister's house with her two children and the uncertainty of what the future held for her, indeed for us all, with this new development.

I had hired a car to take me, my daughter and her daughters to Heathrow airport. I'd left my car with my son in Cardiff for him to use until my return in

January 2017. The journey down was uneventful, we were excited about our adventure but felt sad and guilty about leaving my other daughter especially with the uncertainty of whether she would be granted a visa and of course she had no family support as we had now all gone. A very difficult time for us all. Especially her!

We arrived at the airport and eventually managed to find our car rental location to drop of the car. A shuttle bus took us to our departure terminal, our bags were checked in, all good, then I realised I had left my mobile phone in the hire car. I managed to contact the hire company and they managed to locate the vehicle I'd used and told me my mobile would be brought in on the next shuttle bus. I had to meet it at the place where we had been dropped off. Easier said than done. With my total lack of direction this was a bit of a worrying prospect for me in a very busy airport. I left my daughter and grandchildren to go in search of the shuttle bus always in the knowledge that in that huge area of Heathrow I actually might never meet up with them again. I have to say also at this point that time wasn't on my side either as our plane was boarding. But I was reunited with my phone and our epic journey began.

We arrived at Los Angeles airport about 1am and

located the stand where the hotel bus was going to collect us to take us to our hotel. Many hotel shuttle buses arrived and left, none of which was ours. After waiting for well over an hour, at last, our bus arrived. We were exhausted and fed up by this time and were very relieved to see our bus finally arrive. Unfortunately, there was only room for one passenger. My daughter, along with all our luggage was loaded on and I was informed that another bus would be along in twenty minutes. An hour later, me, along with my granddaughters, got onto the next bus! Not the best start. The hotel reception staff were full of apologies for our long wait and gave us each a free bottle of water in way of compensation!

We were only staying in Los Angeles for two nights and for me that was enough. Lovely place I dare say if that's your thing, but it wasn't mine. We did the usual things, including Disney of course, but I was keen to move on to Fiji, our next stop.

Fiji was wonderful, beautiful, relaxing and tranquil. We spent four nights there and enjoyed it very much. The only strange thing there was the fact that for some reason I seemed to have lost all sense of how to dress. I made up combinations that looked quite ridiculous, so much so that my daughter had to have a word with me, that's when she could stop laughing.

After another lengthy flight our next destination was New Zealand. We arrived in the early hours on a Friday morning and my son-in-law collected us from the airport. He had already been in New Zealand for about six weeks by that time. We all packed into his vehicle and went straight to bed at his newly rented house.

First thing Friday morning after a few hours' sleep my son-in-law took us to a beach café for breakfast at the edge of the Pacific Ocean. We knew we had made the right move to come to this beautiful country.

CHAPTER 34

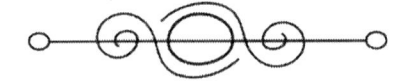

I first went to New York in March 2003. This was halfway between mine and my friend's fiftieth birthdays and we had been saving up for the trip for over a year.

Another friend of mine heard we were planning to go and asked if she could come along. Against our better judgement we agreed, three is not always a good number! The friend that I had originally planned to go with suggested she ask another friend of hers to join us, someone I didn't know particularly well, but we felt four would be a better number than three. So there we were, what had originally started out as me and my very close friend going together to New York, turned out to be four of us, and we didn't all know each other particularly well. But it turned out fine and we all got along although it wasn't quite what we had originally planned. We did all the usual things, sightseeing etc, although when we went on the boat to see the Statue of Liberty, I must have been looking in the wrong direction and missed it! We went to see a show on Broadway and took the city loop bus and saw all the famous landmarks. On the flight out I managed to spill coffee onto my tray which in turn dribbled through the gap and I ended up with a very unsightly brown patch on my white trousers all around the crotch area. Not a good look. No matter!!

However, some five years later another friend of mine and I decided to go to New York together, and we had a ball. For once – and very unusually for me – everything went unbelievable and amazingly well. Everything we did during our stay turned out to be jaw droppingly fantastic. In fact we could only conclude that we were being mistaken for someone else! We couldn't put a foot wrong.

It started when we arrived at JFK airport. As we made our way towards the yellow cabs, a guy approached us and said he had just dropped off a fare in his stretch limo and would take us into the city for the same price as a yellow cab. We were a bit gobsmacked, but he did. He also gave us his card to ring him and said he would take us back to the airport at the same rate – which he did!

We arrived at our hotel, which was fabulous, to check-in and were immediately upgraded to a super-duper room. One where if you needed the bathroom in the night, some blue LED floor lights came on as you got out of bed and lit your way to the bathroom. I was very impressed.

We decided to have our first breakfast in the hotel restaurant then go out to eat breakfast the other four mornings as it was $28 each and we felt that was a bit expensive. But as my friend approached the reception desk to make a general enquiry she was given vouchers for complimentary breakfasts for the duration of our trip. Amazing!

We then went out to do some exploring. As we had both been to New York before we didn't need to do the usual sightseeing trips, so we mooched about and went into Macy's. As soon as we approached one of the make-up counters, a lovely lady invited us to both have a complimentary facial, and booked us in for the following day!

We decided to take a walk through Central Park and wore appropriate clothing and shoes for such a venture, instead of our usual heels etc. After a couple of hours and feeling a bit weary and in need of a drink, we went into a fabulous looking hotel. As we felt a little underdressed from our Central Park excursion, we approached the bar and asked if we were ok to get a drink there. We were assured that we were absolutely fine. As we were deciding what drink to have, a very elegant looking man made a beeline towards us and told the woman serving behind the bar to 'give the ladies whatever they want' and to put it on his tab. He exchanged a few words with us and then disappeared. Well we were both incredulous – who was he? Why had he done that? And who did he think we were? We never did find out any answers to the above, but we had a wonderful afternoon.

That evening we decided to visit a jazz club and lined up in a long queue waiting to be admitted. A security guy who was standing at the door allowing people in and out, approached us, took us to the front of the queue and ushered us in. He then moved some people from a table at the front of the area where the band were playing to give us the best seats in the place… unbelievable. I mean, what was happening, who the hell did they think we were? We just couldn't believe our good fortune and had permanent huge grins on our faces. It was great.

One evening we went to see 'Billy Elliot' on

Broadway, which was absolutely amazing – although the lady in the seat in front of us did fall asleep! Back at our hotel we stopped by the cocktail bar and ordered some drinks. There was a huge mirror behind the bar and as we sat on our stools, we noticed two very attractive men looking our way. After a few more drinks and feeling giddy for a variety of reasons, our good fortune and cocktails being the main ones, these men approached us and asked if we wanted to join them in their room for drinks as the bar was about to close. Surprisingly their room was on the same floor as ours and we had a great time chatting and drinking until the early hours. It seems they were in New York to be on the news the following morning to promote some product they had invented. True to their word, they were on CNN news the next day and invited us out to dinner that night. We all had a great time, they were true gentlemen and didn't let us pay for a thing.

On the last day of our visit we were meeting up with a friend of my friend's daughter who now lived in New York with her husband. We met on a rooftop bar of one of the department stores. She approached us with a bottle of champagne, courtesy of her husband. We had a fabulous afternoon. The sun was beaming down on us as we ordered a further two or three more bottles of champagne as the hours ticked by. It was a fabulous end to what had been the most amazing few days.

I don't think I will ever visit New York again. I could never recreate what we had experienced in those few days when we felt like celebrities. A fantastic memory, and one that I will never ever forget.

We had planned to rent out our houses when we both retired, this friend and me, and hire a van and travel Route 66. Unfortunately my friend had quite a severe stroke at age fifty-nine and has been left quite incapacitated. She is the most amazing lady I know and although physically disabled to a degree has learned to drive again and lives her life to the full. Her spirit is as strong as ever, so is her optimism. I admire her greatly. Her stroke has had a profound effect upon me, partly because our birthdays are only one day apart and I realise every day how fortunate I am and that it can all be taken away in the blink of an eye.

CHAPTER 35

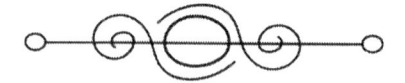

We had been in New Zealand for four days and were having what had become our usual stroll along the beach which was a mere five minutes' walk from our house. We were coming to terms with the beauty and splendour of our location in this lovely seaside resort in the South Island. We loved being beside the Pacific Ocean with the magnificent snow-capped mountains on the horizon. On this particular morning, as it was a weekday, the beach was pretty much deserted and me, my daughter and two grandchildren were meandering along the beach. The children weren't due to start school until the following week. It was a bright sunny day, very peaceful – perfect to recover from our lengthy flights of a few days earlier.

We had just passed by the café on the beach where we'd had our first breakfast the previous Friday morning. As we passed by the café there was a rivulet of water seemingly coming from under a small bridge and making its way to the sea. There was a young mum just ahead of us holding a very young baby in her arms and a toddler was following behind her. The toddler started to paddle in this, what initially looked like, an innocuous shallow pool of water. All of a sudden the toddler totally disappeared into this water and was completely submerged. As I was the nearest person to the child I went to grab him out. I waded in and managed to lift him out of the water and he was able to take in some air. At that point my feet slipped in the mud beneath me and the child was once again faced down in the water completely submerged once more. I was sat in the water up to my neck and couldn't regain my footing. My daughter then lunged towards where she thought the toddler was submerged and felt for an arm or leg and hoisted him out of the water. He was in a terrible state and so was his mum who'd been standing by, shaking and crying and unable to do anything because of the small baby she was holding. I managed to get myself out, covered in mud and silt from top to bottom.

We were all very traumatised by the event and what could have been a situation with a very different outcome. We told ourselves that if for no other reason, we had come to New Zealand to save a little person's life, as we were in no doubt that he would have drowned without us being there just at the right time. Me and my daughter walked slowly home reliving every minute of our drama and unable to stop talking about it for the remainder of the day, until my oldest granddaughter rolled her eyes and asked us how many more times were we going to keep going over it. We did stop at that point but it's strange when you've had a traumatic event how you have to keep going over it until it's been expunged to some extent.

Unfortunately my mobile phone, which was in my handbag, which had been over my shoulder when I plunged into the water, never recovered! It was totally waterlogged and even after putting it into a bag of rice for a week I had to accept, alas, it couldn't be saved. I was gutted actually as all my contacts with friends and family across the other side of the world had been lost. Still, small price to pay I guess in the scheme of things.

CHAPTER 36

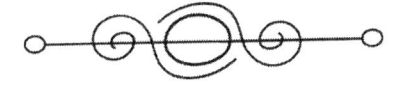

The plan was for me to live with my family whilst in New Zealand as I could only stay for six months due to visa restrictions. I shared a room with my granddaughter which was great fun and worked wonderfully well. We would chat and laugh well into the night and my daughter would have to come in to the bedroom on many occasions to tell us both off.

My other son-in-law had rented a beautiful house on a hill with panoramic views overlooking the village and the ocean, in preparation for his family's arrival. There was a separate self-contained living area for me to stay with him and my daughter and their children when and if she arrived. For me to move in there with him before my daughter arrived from the UK seemed a little inappropriate.

The next few weeks were both wonderful and difficult. We were exploring and acclimatising to our new home and loved every minute of it, but it was awkward when speaking to the daughter who had been left behind, as it was still uncertain as to whether she would be granted her visa so it would have been a little indelicate to say how much we loved the place and going on about all our new experiences. But thankfully, and after a five-week agonising wait since our departure, she finally was granted her visa. What relief and joy.

I moved into my new living space and let my granddaughter have her bedroom back. Although I must say both of us had been perfectly happy with the existing arrangement.

CHAPTER 37

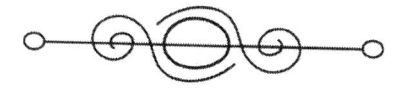

I thoroughly enjoyed every minute of my six-month stay in New Zealand. Waking up to that spectacular view was so replenishing for the soul and gave a wonderful sense of wellbeing. I loved the luxury of space, the feeling of breathing in fresh air and the relaxed atmosphere. But most of all I loved how welcoming and non-judgmental the people I met seemed to be. Individuality and quirkiness seemed to be embraced, and I loved that. I also loved the fact that people of all ages mixed so well together. Being an older person didn't make me feel marginalised in any way or on the periphery at any get together. I found that very refreshing. But what suited me very well and I really enjoyed was the fact that the people I met over there are quite direct. I don't mean rude or offensive in any way, but straight talking and that's how I like to be and I loved that. As you may have realised from my writing so far, I don't go in for 'padding' or 'waffling'. Just direct and to the point – that's how I like it.

So all in all the New Zealand lifestyle suits me very well, and on every level, and I am looking forward to hopefully being able to be there permanently in a few years' time. It surprises me actually how easily I have adapted to my new situation. For one, I don't have the security of my own home anymore, something I had been used to all my adult life. I wasn't working, something else I had always done and I actually wasn't the one in control of events so to speak. I was living in my daughter's house and all things domestic now came under her jurisdiction. I helped out of course, and we came to an arrangement that I'd be the 'house person' ie tidying, cleaning, ironing, etc so long as I didn't have to cook! And as both my daughters were trying to establish themselves in the work market, I happily plugged the gaps. I'd often accompany one or other of my daughters when they did their weekly shop, but all choices and decisions were mainly down to them. One time when I went supermarket shopping with one of my girls we couldn't remember where we had parked the car or which exit to leave by (the supermarket was in a large shopping mall) and spent more than twenty minutes pushing a supermarket trolley laden with bargains, my daughter was on a tight budget, through the shopping mall - something I would have found excruciatingly embarrassing back in the UK, but who cares? This was a different life and it just seemed ridiculously funny at the time.

The days passed by effortlessly. There were local coffee shops to sample, regular walks along the beach and the little local cinema to frequent on a dismal afternoon when my daughters were busy and I had time to spare. Although I lived with one of my daughters I had two sleepovers a week at my other daughter's house, it was great. I'd sometimes take or collect my grandchildren to and from school which was always a joy. As the weather turned hotter we would spend a lot of time in the outdoor school swimming pool which was available to village residents. Like most other pool users, we would take some food and drinks and make an occasion out of it.

From first arriving in our village resort we fell into the habit of every Saturday afternoon spending a couple of hours at a local bar with a large outside decked area on to the beach overlooking the sea. The kids played on the beach while we chatted and had a few drinks. I felt like I was on a permanent holiday, and I suppose I was. Maybe that's what retirement feels like.

Halloween was a strange affair, trick or treating in broad daylight! After a few house calls with the kids I decided to set myself up outside my daughter's house, in full witch's outfit, with a bottle of wine and bowls of goodies for any child brave enough to approach me. It was great fun. Bonfire night was equally strange as again fireworks in the daylight with the sun beating down did lose some of its magic.

Christmas was always going to be unusual too. No-one wants a traditional roast turkey dinner with all the trimmings in the baking hot mid-summer. We settled on barbequed food on the patio with a variety of salads and other delicacies. Lovely in its own way, but for me not really a proper Christmas. I must say, perhaps because of over sixty Christmases in the winter, with curtains drawn and candles lit, I found it unusual and not in a good way, and not something I will ever get used to I don't think. I like a cosy traditional Christmas in the winter time. What I did like about a New Zealand Christmas though is that it's very much lower key than back in the UK, where I feel it's total saturation for three months prior to the main event.

One of my sons came over on a holiday for three weeks in the October of 2016 and we took a trip to a hot springs resort. It was great fun experiencing the different natural pools. While we were there we also went on a jet boat and quad bikes. I absolutely loved those bikes. I had decided back in the dreadful year of 2014 that I was going to be a 'yes' person and have as many new experiences as I could handle, within reason. I draw the line at bungy jumping!

As I said, Christmas day was very different to what I'm used to, but on Christmas Eve we had a ball. My youngest daughter had arranged for a group of us to meet on the beach. We all took food and drinks. We set up a gazebo and my daughter had organised a quiz and some beach games. It really was a brilliant day.

CHAPTER 38

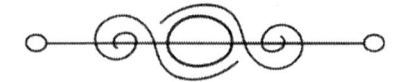

As Christmas in New Zealand is in the school summer holidays we did what most people do, and went on holiday on Boxing Day. There were both my daughters and their families and me. We had decided to go camping. We were to spend the first two nights in a very basic location by a lake, with the only facilities being a toilet block. We were then moving on to a more civilized location for three nights and then ending up at Lake Tekapo over the New Year for the remaining three nights. Eight nights in all, under canvas! Five adults, four children and a dog. We packed two vehicles to the gunnels, food, clothing, bedding, cooking equipment etc and one of my sons-in-law was towing a trailer with a boat attached and numerous bicycles.

Our first location was about a two-and-a-half hours' drive away. When we arrived there were no designated pitches as such, you just found your own space in a clearing. First job was to trample down the grass so we had an area on which to pitch our tent and a gazebo which was to be our cooking area. Having accomplished all this we had a wander down to the lake to check out our location. There were lots of other campers there, I suppose, but because of the way it was set out we didn't see another soul. It had been decided by the grandchildren that to be fair I would have to divide my sleeping time between them equally in each of their tents.

We had our two nights there, and surprisingly, all went well, apart from when my daughter had to take one of her children to the toilet in the dead of night and couldn't find her way back to us. After being gone over half an hour we heard a distant voice calling out and my son-in-law had to try to find them. My daughter said she had tried to remain calm for the sake of her daughter, but was in fact petrified. It was pitch black and there were no landmarks to help guide her back to us. Two nights in such a remote location was enough for us and we were all ready to move on to somewhere with a few more facilities…

in particular a shower block!

We packed everything away and set off on our next epic three to four hour journey to our next stopping place. My daughter at the last minute had decided to take the few remaining bits of food we had left, crackers, cheese and few biscuits – thank goodness she did! About two hours into our journey a wheel nut sheared off the trailer which was towing the boat and bikes, and we had to immediately pull over. Thankfully we were just alongside a layby and were able to make a hasty stop. Unfortunately, we were in the middle of nowhere and couldn't get a signal on any of our mobile phones. After assessing the situation it was clear we needed assistance. Both my sons-in-law headed off in one of the vehicles to find a spot where they could pick up a signal for the mobile phones to try to get some help. They had been gone about half an hour and arrived back to say help was on its way, but that it would be another hour or so before anyone could get out to us. That's when the cheese and crackers and remaining biscuits came into their own.

We decided that it was not necessary for us all to hang about awaiting assistance so the decision was made that both my daughters along with three of the children would continue on to the next site, while me, my two sons-in-law and my eldest granddaughter waited with the vehicle and trailer. Help eventually arrived and the guy did manage to do a 'make do' job to sort us out for the remainder of our trip but said that it would need repairing properly when we got back home. He also had to use the spare tyre. The spare tyre was flat and the mechanic unfortunately didn't have a pump on his vehicle. So he, along with my son-in-law and myself went in search of a local farmer friend of his to inflate the spare tyre. Eventually we got on our way and arrived at our next destination. The girls had done their best to put up our tents and gazebo but nothing looked quite as it should but the fellas soon managed to sort it out. What a day. We were all a bit weary by this time, but food had to be cooked and cleared away before we could call it a day.

It had been very windy during that night and by morning the gazebo was looking a little dishevelled. But as this was unusual for the time of year, we were hopeful all would be well for the rest of our stay there. Unfortunately, all was not well and the next night the 'unusual' wind took its final revenge on our poor unsuspecting gazebo and the whole frame was buckled and unusable. We had to pack away our crippled gazebo unfortunately, which was a shame really as it had been a good place to store and cook our food.

I must say, we had a good time whilst we were there in spite of the mishap with the gazebo. We went gold panning in a disused mine, we watched the bungy jumping, which two of my granddaughters wanted to do but weren't old enough, thankfully, and we had a fabulous trip into Queenstown. My eldest granddaughter and me opted for a trip on a lovely steamship to visit an old farmhouse to have afternoon tea, see the animals and watch the sheep shearing, while the others all chose to go up on a very high cable car. Not our idea of fun. We met up again after our separate jaunts and had a lovely meal together in a very friendly restaurant. The next day we packed up once again and moved on to our last stop for the last three nights of our trip.

Our final destination was the most luxurious, with hot pools and free lakeside barbeques to use. We ate a delicious meal on New Year's Eve and went to bed. That night the wind was blowing a gale and this time it was more than our tents could cope with. All our tent poles buckled. The noise was scary and the kids were screaming as the wind howled and the canvas was flapping uncontrollably. Me and my granddaughter had to relocate to the car. My daughter, husband and other granddaughter sought refuge in the other car. My other daughter and her family managed to stay in their tent as the bedroom areas were intact but the tent had ripped off the poles of the 'communal' area of their tent. I've never spent a New Year's Eve quite like it, sleeping in a car, but it was fine. We had an inflatable airbed and could see the sky through the sun roof. We quite enjoyed it actually, far better than staying in that collapsed tent.

The following morning, my daughter and family who had managed to remain in their tent for the night, decided that they'd had enough and packed up to go back home. As their tent had been partially damaged they decided to abandon it, but as the two bedroom compartments were still intact I suggested that we use it and stay the remaining night, just so we could say we had done it and not to be beaten! And so we did. Eight nights under canvas, what an experience, not one I care to repeat any time soon, but an experience nevertheless.

CHAPTER 39

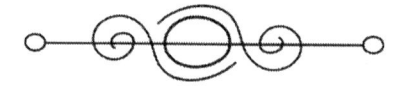

I had to return to the UK in the January of 2017 as I could only stay for six months and my time was almost up. My return flight was booked for 16th January. It was going to be an emotional time saying my goodbyes for the next nine months or so until I could return to New Zealand. Me and my daughters and their children had seen each other virtually every single day of our lives so it was going to be tough. But I was also really looking forward to reuniting with both my sons back in the UK, my other five grandchildren and my many good friends. So the day of my departure was a day of very mixed emotions.

I had spent the previous week wrapping and packing away all the items of mine that were staying in New Zealand as I knew it was highly likely that the daughter I was living with would have moved house during my absence and wanted to lighten her burden and not have her and my son-in-law having to sort out my belongings as well as their own.

An hour before I was due to set off to the airport I received a phone call from my brother back in England telling me that our mum had just passed away. As I said... a day of very mixed emotions. My mother was ninety-three and had dementia for the last year or so of her life. In fact that was why I felt able to leave England and stay away for so long, as by the time I left in July of 2016 she really didn't know me anymore and was in a care home.

Although I hadn't been there at the very end of her life and had in effect said my goodbyes to her when I left for New Zealand, knowing that her time was nearing its end, I was desperate to arrive back in time to attend her funeral. I was due to arrive at Heathrow airport at 6am on Tuesday 17th and my son was collecting me from the airport. He lived only twenty minutes or so drive away at that time, and my mother's funeral was to take place on the following day. So after a long, gruelling and emotional flight back to the UK I then had a four-hour drive north the next day for my mum's funeral.

As I had sold my house before leaving for New Zealand the plan was for me to stay with my son who lived in Cardiff for the time I was back in the UK. He had rented a house there for us both on his return from holidaying in New Zealand the previous November. He picked me up from his brother's house on the Saturday following the funeral. I found it a bit tough getting used to life in Cardiff. I didn't know my way around and apart from my son, his boys and his ex-partner, I didn't know a soul, and it was winter!

But life took on a routine of sorts. I've always been an early riser and would be up around 6.30am and was able to make my son a packed lunch for his day at work and have a coffee ready for him when he woke a short time after me. He didn't need me to do those things of course, but it made me feel a bit useful, and as I suddenly had a lot of time of my hands, I kept our little place in order and did the usual 'housey' things.

I found it difficult initially getting used to long days alone with nothing much to occupy my time. In fact it's true to say that spending long periods totally alone with nothing much to do is my idea of hell and is my Achilles heel actually. When I was working at my salon, I loved and relished the peace and quiet of evenings on my own in my little house. I also enjoyed quiet mornings too and getting up with no-one else around. But suddenly I was thrust into having many daytime hours with nothing particularly to do and no-one I could just call upon to meet up with and have a chat. I found it challenging.

Looking back it is something I am glad I had to face. I have realised I can do it, and although it's not something I would choose to do again, I know I can. Surprisingly, towards the end of my stay in Cardiff I had actually become accustomed to my new way of life and although it wasn't a very stimulating or fulfilling life style for me, I had settled in to it. Although my life there was sometimes a bit boring I never got depressed or down about it and that's what I had dreaded most. On the upside, my grandsons stayed with us every weekend and that was a great joy. Having never lived in the same city as the boys, our visits were only four or five times a year, so it was wonderful to bond with them and to get to know them better.

During my time in Cardiff I did return to my home town of Sheffield quite regularly where I was able to stay at my son and daughter-in-law's house - they had bought a house there by then – and spend time with my two young granddaughters and catch up with my friends, whom I'd missed dearly.

It was whilst I was in Cardiff that the lady who was managing my salon (with a view to taking it over after a period of two years) dropped the bombshell that she didn't want to continue looking after the place and definitely didn't want to take it over. I was a bit shell-shocked actually and spent a couple of sleepless nights coming to terms with her news and trying to work out a solution. Thankfully I was back in the UK at least to sort it out. Although her news was a bit of a shock and totally unexpected it would have been a real nightmare had I still been in New Zealand.

So, once the news had been digested and I'd got over the initial surprise of her decision it was time to put out feelers to see who wanted to by a beauty/nails and hair salon! There had been a woman who I had trained many years earlier and who had worked for me for a year or so back in the day. We had kept a loose contact through social media, and she lived very close to my salon.

I knew she had her own small salon above a shop a fair distance away from where she lived and that she was a 'one man band' so to speak. I decided to message her and let her know my salon was going up for sale. She might just be interested… a long shot but worth a try. I sent her a private message asking if she might be interested in buying my place. I didn't really hold out much hope of success, I mean what were the chances? Well she messaged me back saying she would be interested in having a chat about it. We met up and had our chat. I had written down some figures 'on the back of a fag packet'… not literally. She said she would speak to her husband and get back to me. She also informed me that her aunt's house sale was completing on the Friday of that week and that she was the sole beneficiary – it was Wednesday!! We were both a bit excited, she felt maybe it was meant to be. She wasn't too happy where she was currently, the area was a bit rundown and she couldn't get any passing trade due to being above a shop. Also her aunt's house had been empty for five years and a sale was only now going through. Maybe it was part of some grand pre-ordained plan. Maybe her aunt with whom she was very close was watching over her. I certainly felt someone was watching over me. And there we are. Exactly two weeks after my manager said she wanted out of the business it was taken over and I was done with it. It felt like a great relief to be free of it. Having said that, I loved every minute of my almost twenty years of owning my salon and working in the business. But living half my life at the other side of the world for a few years, and planning to make New Zealand my home in the future, it only made sense to end that particular phase of my life.

CHAPTER 40

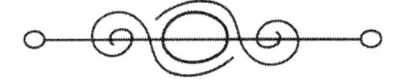

One of my first trips out of Cardiff was to see my sister and her family in Norwich, an altogether lengthy and horrendous journey. I did look into flying there, but it took about nineteen hours with a stopover in Geneva or some such place!!

I decided to break up the journey and spend a couple of nights in Sheffield, visit my dentist, then continue on to Norwich. Most of my subsequent visits to my home town included a visit to the dentist. This isn't because my teeth are bad in any way, in fact quite the contrary, they are straight, clean and pretty good I'd say. But just before I left for New Zealand I had decided to have an implant in my lower right jaw which would enable me to chew on both sides of my mouth. As I had some spare cash with having sold my house I thought it was a good opportunity to sort myself out a bit, and this necessitated numerous dental appointments.

I had also decided to see about having a breast reduction. I had always been very 'healthy' in the breast department and finally decided I'd had enough of lugging them around. I did once enquire about getting a reduction done on the NHS but I didn't quite meet the criteria – BMI too high due to being a tad overweight alas. Part of my visit to see my sister was to have a consultation there at a private clinic where my sister said she would be able to look after me during my recuperation and we would be able to spend a decent amount of time together after my lengthy absence.

I arrived at my sister's house a couple of days prior to my consultation where she had said she would accompany me. On the morning of my consultation, my sister set off to her place of work. Using the satnav on my mobile phone I would drive to her work and she would then drive us to the clinic for me to meet with the consultant.

It was while taking a shower on the morning of my consultation I decided it was suddenly vitally important that I shave my legs. I don't know why I made that decision really, as they weren't particularly in need of shaving and the consultant clearly wouldn't be examining anything below the naval. Still the seed had been sown and it was suddenly imperative that I had freshly shaved legs. Just as I bent down to start the shaving process I heard a sharp snapping sound and my back had 'gone'. Now my back does 'go' periodically – nothing seems to set it off, but when it does happen it can take many days of me walking like a primate, unable to stand fully upright before it eases off, and I am able to function normally again. However this seemed different. I felt something actually ping and I couldn't straighten up – at all. It was excruciatingly painful, but the kind of pain that sometimes makes you laugh because it is all so comical and ridiculous.

So I am stranded in my sister's house, alone, in the shower, and not knowing how I am actually going to get out. And I have an appointment with my consultant in less than two hours' time. With extreme difficulty and with a few abortive attempts and with much grunting and groaning like I had Tourette's, I managed to struggle, soaking wet and covered in soap, out of the shower. I located my mobile phone and tried contacting my sister to let her know of my predicament. Unfortunately my mobile had no signal, and I could only assume no credit, which in itself was strange as I was on a contract… no matter. I struggled around her house trying to find a landline handset. On finding her house phone I realised that I didn't know her mobile number, so back again to retrieve my mobile to get her number. Time was slipping away fast as all of this took some considerable time and I was still clad only in a towel and didn't know how I would be able to get dressed unaided. As my mobile phone seemed out of action and I wouldn't be able to use the satnav, my sister suggested she ring a taxi to pick me up and take me to her work place. So all I had to do was get dressed. No mean feat. Eventually dressed the only other hurdle was to negotiate the stairs and climb into the taxi. It wasn't easy but I managed. The taxi driver assumed I was disabled but didn't offer any assistance, which to be honest, wouldn't have helped.

I struggled into my sister's car and we were both laughing (and me moaning) uncontrollably. My sister informed me, belatedly, that I wouldn't have been able to get a phone signal in the room I was staying in. Thanks for that, so my satnav would have worked!

We duly arrived at the clinic. Me bent almost double and both of us laughing at the absurdity of it all. We were shown in to the consultant's rooms whereupon I had to point out that although my breasts were quite heavy, they didn't cause me to walk the way I was currently and that I did usually walk quite upright. After a ten minute question and answer session I had to remove my upper clothing and sit on the couch so he could examine me and take some measurements. My sister was sat directly in front of me observing the proceedings when my mobile started to ring. My sister answered my phone and I could hear her outlining to my close friend just what was taking place. As we all giggled like silly kids the consultant thankfully maintained his professionalism.

CHAPTER 41

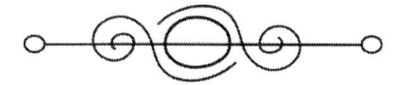

Something eventful often occurred when visiting my sister – and not always in a good way. There was one occasion when me, my daughter and her two children spent Easter weekend at my sister's house. My daughter and her husband were not living together at the time and we thought a little break would do us all good. My daughter was a little apprehensive about the visit as her children were quite young and my sister's house is not – let's say – child friendly. Everything in her house is of a very high standard and is always pristine, but although I'm guessing my brother-in-law was a little reticent about our impending visit, my sister assured us it would all be fine. To be fair my brother-in-law was brilliant with the children and had put a lot of effort into making an Easter egg hunt for them in their beautiful garden.

It was rather unfortunate therefore when one of my granddaughters, probably having had too many chocolate eggs, was sick on their beautiful winter white shag pile bedroom carpet. My brother-in-law did his best and shot upstairs with a well-stocked cleaning caddy, but to no avail, the carpet never fully recovered and remained crusty in places until they felt they had to buy a replacement. Thankfully the new carpet wasn't purchased until my other daughter and her two children accompanied us on what was becoming an annual visit, and her daughter was also sick on the same bedroom carpet! I don't recall my daughters and their children ever visiting again. No-one felt totally relaxed and comfortable visiting from then on.

I had to commit to having my breast reduction surgery by four months from my initial consultation, which meant I had until June to make my decision whether or not to proceed. It was a procedure I really did want and saw no reason why it would not happen.

Unfortunately... best made plans and all that!!

My sister and me, although we have never seen each other all that often over the years due to busy lives, commitments with work and family and living in different cities, we have always been close and when we are together have the best of times and get on like a house on fire. It was therefore extremely upsetting that we had a falling out over a money issue. There is no need for me to expand on that other than to say I realised it would be impossible for me to have my surgery and stay at her house. About three weeks after our disagreement we resolved our differences and misunderstanding and our relationship resumed as it had always been thankfully. But it was during our period of 'falling out', though, that I decided to have lens replacement surgery instead of a breast reduction. It did make more sense really as I'd reached the stage where I was constantly changing my face furniture depending on whether I was reading, driving or sitting in the sun. Driving in sunshine meant I switched from specs to contact lenses so I could wear my sunglasses, altogether an unsatisfactory situation.

CHAPTER 42

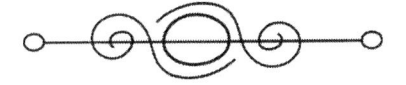

I had seen an advertisement on social media listing all the positives of laser treatment or lens replacement surgery. Although this was, up until that point, not something I had ever considered or even been aware of particularly, I was extremely interested. I gave them a call. An appointment was made for me to have an eye examination and to see which procedure would be of the most benefit to me. Needless to say it was the more expensive replacement lenses that would be my best option. Had I have chosen the laser treatment I would still need to wear glasses for certain things, which seemed pointless and rather defeated the object of the exercise, I thought. As I was living in Cardiff at this time and although laser treatment could be carried out there, I would need to travel to Bristol for the more intricate lens replacement surgery.

My left eye was to be done on the morning of my arrival and my right eye was getting sorted the following day, so I booked into a nearby hotel for an overnight stay. I had travelled by train from Cardiff to Bristol early on the morning of my surgery and my son was going to collect me by car the following day when it was all complete. Driving myself there and back was clearly not going to be an option!

I was filled with a certain amount of trepidation as I travelled to Bristol for my first eye surgery. I had been told, in detail, exactly what would be involved and it wasn't a pleasant prospect. I must say, though, that the thought of eye surgery was far worse than the actual procedure. That being said, it wasn't exactly pleasant. It certainly wasn't painful in any way but it was a very strange sensation and makes most people feel rather squeamish when I tell them I had it done. I hadn't seen the need for anyone to accompany me to Bristol but the staff at the clinic seemed a little concerned that no-one was meeting me after my first eye surgery was completed. I realise why now actually. My left eye had a dressing over it and a plastic 'bug like' shield, but I still needed my glasses to have clear vision in my right, as yet, untreated eye. I must have looked a right sight making my way gingerly to my hotel. Thankfully it was only a short distance from the clinic. The worst part of the whole day for me was when I had to take off the dressing some four hours later and put three lots of eye drops into my recently treated eye at five minute intervals. I found it quite worrying that the vision in that eye was virtually non-existent, as I had been expecting an immediate improvement and I spent a very disturbed night concerned that the procedure hadn't gone to plan. The following morning however reasonable vision had been restored and it was panic over. I was good to go and get my right eye done.

Having that eye surgery was one of the best decisions I have ever made and would recommend it to anyone. It's totally liberating. I'll just have to lug my boobs around a little longer!!

CHAPTER 43

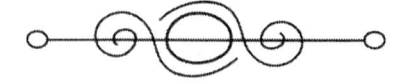

As I previously mentioned, I made many trips back to my home town of Sheffield whilst living in Cardiff on my return to the UK, and many of these trips did involve visits to the dentist. I had started my tooth implant treatment just prior to leaving the UK for my six month stay in New Zealand. On my return to the UK I was ready for the next part of my implant procedure. The next stage involved x-rays and taking impressions of my teeth. The following visit would be to have the implant inserted once it had been made and the whole procedure would be complete.

Whenever I made a follow-up appointment at the dentist I would mention that I would be travelling three to four hours to attend, so the staff there were well aware of this situation and in fact commented that I was the furthest away patient geographically, that they had. An appointment was made for the final stage of my procedure and I received the usual courtesy text reminding me of my appointment time and date. I was looking forward to it all being over and done with as these long distance appointments were a bit of a pain.

I arrived at the dentist twenty minutes or so ahead of my appointment time and waited to be called in for my final visit. The time of my appointment passed and no-one called me. Ten minutes passed and then twenty, and still I wasn't called in for my scheduled appointment. I spoke to the receptionist and asked why there was a delay. Half an hour after my appointment time was due, my dentist approached me and asked me to take a seat... in his office. Very strange, why wasn't I going into the dentist chair?!

After much head scratching, leafing through notes and profuse apologies, it emerged that the wrong tooth had been sent and I had in fact been given Ian's!! Who the hell was Ian – and had he got my tooth? It would have all been quite humorous if I hadn't just used a tank of petrol, set off at some ungodly hour and driven for three-and-a-half hours to make my noon appointment. Still there was nothing that could be done and another appointment was scheduled for three weeks later and at that time the whole procedure was complete.

I was reimbursed for my tank of petrol on a wasted journey and presented with a huge bouquet of flowers when we said our final goodbyes. I left the flowers with a friend in Sheffield. I didn't think our little house in Cardiff could easily accommodate them.

CHAPTER 44

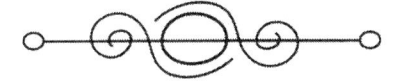

When I first arrived in Cardiff in the January of 2017, my son had ordered a bed for me but there had been an unexpected delay of two weeks or so for the delivery. In the meantime I slept on two sofas pushed together which resembled a rather large dog bed. In actual fact, I found this arrangement quite comfortable and insisted my son cancel the order for the bed. I was only going to be there for nine months after all, and it suited me fine. It did make me laugh some nights though when I went to my bedroom, yes I had a bedroom, and I had to sit on the side and sort of roll in.

Whilst I was in the UK it made sense for my daughter to make use of my little VW beetle during my absence. She hadn't needed to use the car for the first couple of months I was away. She did need to use it, though, in about April as she had just secured a new job and needed the car to get her to the training sessions she was about to begin which were some way away from where she lived.

As she set off on her journey on day one of her training course, there was an unexpected and very loud sound like gunshots which came from the back of the car. The back window had unexpectedly and completely exploded. It gave her quite a shock I can tell you. She was starting a new job in a location she was unfamiliar with and it was all rather traumatic and not the best start to a day when she was already a little nervous about the newness of everything.

I must say, I was very impressed with the insurance company I used in New Zealand. As my car was a convertible it wasn't going to be a simple job of replacing the rear window. In fact, the whole roof had to be replaced at considerable expense and as the insurance company couldn't find a replacement roof in New Zealand, they located one in Germany and had it shipped over. Amazing!

Now, I'm not a huge fan of technology, it is most probably an age thing, but I must say that being at the other end of the world to some of my immediate family at any given time it has been a godsend. Being able to keep in touch through messaging and facetime or Skype has been fantastic. It was during one of these regular calls that my youngest daughter told me she needed to get copies of both her and her husband's birth certificates and their marriage certificate. They had moved house whilst I was back in the UK and couldn't find these documents that they urgently needed.

I set about contacting the main government building where these documents are held and gave all the necessary details they would need, names, dates of births etc, or so I thought. There was to be an inflated fee to be paid for these copy documents to be fast tracked, which I duly paid. They were urgently required after all! I subsequently received an email saying that there was no trace of a birth certificate for my daughter. That was very strange. I decided to contact the register office in the city where she had been born, but again, no record of her. I then remembered that we had in fact 'tweaked' and altered our surname a couple of times over the years and I couldn't really remember what name we had been using at the time of her birth. Feeling rather foolish and embarrassed, I gave the very helpful lady at the other end of the phone a couple of options to try and my daughter was at last found. She did exist. I knew she did all along. I was delighted at having secured these certificates in record time at the cost of only £78!! By the time I received these certificates a couple of day later through the post my daughter told me, panic over. She didn't need them quite as urgently as she had first thought – you've got to laugh, haven't you?

I returned to New Zealand in November 2017. I will be here for nine months on this visit. I'm not sure exactly where I'll be living when I go back to the UK, as the son I lived with in Cardiff, moved out to New Zealand himself in January 2018.

Something will turn up – it always does.

Let the next chapter begin...

ABOUT THE AUTHOR

I have four children and nine grandchildren (so far). I guess I live a strange life by lots of people's standards. I sold my forever house in 2016 at the age of 63 and embarked on a life of flitting between New Zealand and the UK. It actually feels quite liberating because even though my house gave me security, I have discovered that it also kept me trapped, in a strange way.

I have always felt that every stage of my life has been the best. I still feel that. Will I be saying that if I make it another twenty or thirty years, who knows? I'll let you know when I get there.

Printed in Great Britain
by Amazon